To my sisters in the Congregation of St. Joseph
and to all who labor to translate the Gospel
into the word that brings abundant life
to men and women of every age.

# Liturgy and Spirituality in Context:
## Perspectives on Prayer and Culture

Eleanor Bernstein, C.S.J., editor

**THE LITURGICAL PRESS**
Collegeville, Minnesota

Cover illustration by Barbara Schmich. Cover design by Joshua Jeide, O.S.B.

| 1 | 2 | 3 | 4 | 5 | 6 | 7 | 8 | 9 |
|---|---|---|---|---|---|---|---|---|

**Library of Congress Cataloging-in-Publication Data**

Liturgy and spirituality in context : perspectives on prayer and culture /
    Eleanor Bernstein, editor.
        p. cm.
    Includes bibliographical references.
    ISBN 0-8146-1842-1
    1. Catholic Church—Liturgy—Congresses. 2. Christianity and
culture—Congresses. 3. Spirituality—Catholic Church—Congresses.
4. Spirituality—Congresses. 5. Liturgics—Congresses. 6. Catholic
Church—Doctrines—Congresses. I. Bernstein, Eleanor.
BX1970.A1L58  1990                                                          89-77871
261'.1—dc20                                                                        CIP

# Contents

# Contributors

JOHN F. BALDOVIN, s.j., is associate professor of historical and liturgical theology, Jesuit School of Theology and the Graduate Theological Union, Berkeley.

PETER FINK, s.j., is associate professor of sacramental/liturgical theology, Weston School of Theology.

EMILIE GRIFFIN, an author and businesswoman, is the creative director of Duke Unlimited, New Orleans.

ROBERT HOVDA is a retired priest of the Diocese of Fargo and a columnist, writer, and lecturer on issues of ecclesial and liturgical renewal.

MARIA LEONARD is a businesswoman and chairperson of "Christians in the Workplace," St. Clement Parish, Chicago.

M. FRANCIS MANNION is rector of the Cathedral of the Madeleine and diocesan director of theological affairs, Diocese of Salt Lake City.

GERTRUD MUELLER NELSON is an author and artist, Del Mar, California.

DON SALIERS is professor of theology and liturgics, The Candler School of Theology, Emory University.

MARK SEARLE is associate professor of theology, University of Notre Dame.

# Acknowledgments

It is truly right and just to acknowledge with gratitude those who have made possible the publication of these proceedings. Sincere thanks to the writers who, in addition to being speakers at the Notre Dame conferences, agreed to go the extra mile and prepare a paper for future publication. Thanks are also due to David Stosur who first read the papers with me and became a valued dialogue partner, offering helpful insights regarding the relationship and sequence of the topics; to Patrick Malloy, who served as super sleuth and tracked down elusive footnotes; to Lorraine Strope who spent long hours at the typewriter and the copy machine; and to John Brooks-Leonard, trusted colleague, whose ear for language and whose good writing and editing skills made him a valued editor's editor.

# Introduction

Social commentators describe life in these latter years of the twentieth century in many ways—complex, fast-moving, technological,
ambiguous, competitive, individualistic, futuristic. While this book
is not a collection of sociological commentaries on North American
society, it is impossible to consider theological topics like liturgy
and spirituality apart from their social context.

The interrelationship of liturgy and life, of spirituality and culture is fundamental to the Judeo-Christian tradition. It is an age-
old dynamic, recognizable in the great figures of the Old Testament: prophets like Amos and Hosea, Jeremiah and Isaiah were
constantly interpreting the covenant in terms of the daily life of
the covenanted people. Jesus himself, in word and action, sought
to share his vision of a God who was revealed not in abstract
categories but in everyday life. We cannot hope to understand the
Scriptures apart from their social context.

To discuss cultural issues, then, alongside theological questions
is not a revolutionary approach. It is a dialogue that is consistent
with and inseparable from the ongoing growth and development
of the Church throughout its history. Pastoral liturgy stands in
this tradition, firmly committed to the unfolding worship life of
the Christian community as that worship life celebrates and hands
on the faith of generations in the accents of contemporary culture.
Pastoral liturgy is the dialogue between the liturgical tradition and
the contemporary pastoral situation.

This collection of selected papers derives from two recent conferences sponsored by the Notre Dame Center for Pastoral Liturgy:
"Forming the Worship Community: An Owners' Guide" in 1987
and "Liturgy and Spirituality in Dialogue" in 1988. The authors
explore the relationships of culture, spirituality, and liturgy. Three
of the papers—those by Mannion, Searle, and Fink—address the
broad cultural and religious questions that are inherent in these
relationships. The remaining papers deal with various aspects of
liturgy and spirituality: the challenge to interiority, liturgy forming
us in the ways of prayer and Christian living, the liturgical year as
a calendar for a just society, the Christian formation of children,
and the relationship of Sunday to the workweek.

Francis Mannion's paper, "Liturgy and the Present Crisis of
Culture," was first delivered at our conference in 1987. A revision

subsequently appeared in *Worship* magazine in March of 1988 and is reprinted here. Building on the insights of a number of social scientists, Mannion probes the relationship between liturgy and contemporary culture. He investigates what success the renewed liturgy has had generating social and cultural transformation, and the impact of modern culture on the perception and practice of the liturgy. His essay serves as a broad backdrop against which to locate and understand the questions, problems, and challenges of spirituality and liturgy posed by the succeeding authors.

In apparent dialogue with Mannion, Mark Searle begins his article, "Private Religion, Individualistic Society, and Common Worship," by noting key characteristics of our culture with an eye to their effect on religiosity in our society. Searle then reflects on the influence of these cultural traits on liturgical practice and finally urges us "beyond the level of 'shared celebrations' at which we are currently stuck" to what he describes as public worship.

Peter Fink, concerned for the interrelationship between liturgy and spirituality, argues for a spiritual depth to all study and practice of the liturgy and "a liturgical face to any spirituality worthy of the name Christian." He calls particular attention to the individualistic and privatistic strains of our culture that dupe us into choosing models of self-fulfillment and self-development instead of the "transformation of life born of suffering and injustice freely embraced." Further, he warns that efforts to politicize the liturgy are ways of seeking control. It is in face of these dangers that the author judges the intersection of liturgy and spirituality to be both necessary and timely.

The remaining papers of the collection situate specific topics within this broader socio-cultural-religious context. In "Liturgy Teaching Us to Pray," Don Saliers observes, "It is not simply a matter of 'How can liturgy teach us to pray?' but 'How can liturgy teach us to pray in a culture of narcissism which shapes religious sensibility?'" The author echoes the concerns of Peter Fink regarding the overemphasis on a kind of self-awareness, a privatistic spiritual pursuit aimed at developing one's own interior life. Saliers suggests that the basic prayer of the liturgy invites us into a broader context and continues the universal prayer of Jesus Christ thus shaping Christians in an attitude of praise and thanksgiving, a way of being in the world and being in right relationship with the Creator and with all of creation. He illustrates this idea with the Eucharistic Prayer itself, the classic prayer pattern familiar to all Christians.

Emilie Griffin sees the challenge to Christian interiority as a challenge to the imagination. She develops her thesis in five areas: the ways in which our culture discourages Christian prayer, what contemplative prayer requires of us, the transforming power of contemplation, the relationship of contemplation to the liturgy, and the relationship of prayer to the apostolate. Griffin stresses the vital interrelationship of imagination, the solitary prayer of contemplation, and liturgical prayer. She insists that structure and discipline are inseparable from the life of prayer, whatever its form.

John Baldovin begins his article, "The Liturgical Year: Calendar for a Just Community," with reference to the eschatological vision of the kingdom, the reign of God. From that perspective, he asserts that no liturgy which describes itself as Christian can be unconcerned about those things which are obstacles to the coming of the kingdom. Baldovin acknowledges the problem of a liturgical calendar that no longer seems to fit the culture of our modern-day world. He proposes, however, a new starting point for understanding the liturgical year today and explores this new approach in terms of (1) the tension between the already and the not-yet, (2) cultural adaptation and (3) the importance of the saints. In the final section of the paper, he sees the liturgical year as an expression of the Christian vision of justice and peace, a vision celebrated in a community which has made a commitment to work for God's reign.

The household of faith, the domestic church, is the focus of Gertrud Mueller Nelson's essay, "Christian Formation of Children." Daughter of writer Therese Mueller who was influenced by the pioneers of the American liturgical movement at St. John's Abbey in Collegeville, Nelson's creative insights and concrete examples build on her own experience of growing up in a family committed to the liturgy. She contends that authentic Christian formation is a process that incorporates all dimensions of the human person and invites discovery of the creative and poetic Church that uses myth, symbol, and the rhythm of the seasons to form its children in the Christian life. Her convictions are borne out with numerous examples from daily life, feasts and festivals, and the annual cycle of the seasons.

Robert Hovda's well-known passion for the liturgy is expressed again in his challenge that we be converted to *do* the liturgy in such a way that the Sunday celebration itself becomes a fount of formation. He presents five challenges, addressed especially to leaders in liturgical ministry, that he considers essential if we are to release the power of the liturgy: (1) become fluent in the symbol language of worship, (2) cherish the unfinished pilgrim nature of the Church, (3) let tomorrow take care of itself, (4) make the world our home and our project, and (5) absorb the sources for the sake of activating the imagination. Hovda sees this engagement with the elements of our worship as central to the issue of liturgy forming us in the Christian life.

The final paper in this collection—Maria Leonard's—reflects on the relationship between Church and the marketplace, between Sunday and the workweek. She writes from the perspective of a professional businesswoman responding to the challenge of making the connections between faith and work. Leonard is convinced that there are many people seeking a way "to become one in Christ, to become whole." She explores three areas which can help us achieve this wholeness: (1) the understanding of who we are and what we are called to do because of our baptism; (2) the liturgy as the symbolic support of our total life, especially life in the marketplace; and (3) practical means of making the connections between faith and work. This article, coming from outside the academic discipline of theology, provides a valuable and much-needed perspective on the subject.

The papers in this collection, while extending over a broad range of subject matter, intersect in many ways. They express common concerns and present similar challenges. The themes sounded by Mannion in the opening essay find echoes in the succeeding chapters, all of which point to the ongoing dialogue between religion and culture. This dialogue is the very *raison d'etre* of pastoral theology and pastoral liturgy. May this volume encourage us to continue the conversation.

Eleanor Bernstein, C.S.J.

M. Francis Mannion

# Liturgy and the Present Crisis of Culture

The relationship between liturgy and culture continues to be one of the most complex and troublesome issues for the Church as it seeks to advance reform established by the Second Vatican Council. This essay will be concerned with two related aspects of that issue: (1) the degree of success of the modern liturgy in generating social and cultural transformation and (2) the impact of modern culture upon the perception and practice of the liturgy.

Examining the history of liturgy's ability to generate culture helps us to measure whether or not modern liturgy has been successful in bringing about the transformation of today's culture. The work of cultural historian Christopher Dawson, whose writings are the subject of renewed interest today, provides a revealing starting point. In his book *Religion and the Rise of Western Culture*, Dawson says that the origin of Western culture is to be found in the spiritual community which emerged from the ruins of the Roman empire. According to Dawson, this spiritual community, of which the Latin Fathers Ambrose, Augustine, Leo, and Gregory were the progenitors, filled the void created by the fall of the empire and prepared the way for the unified spiritual culture of Western Christendom.[1]

What is interesting in Dawson's analysis is the role that liturgy played in the generation of the new culture. In his view, it was in the liturgy more than anything else that "the whole Christian world, Roman, Byzantine and barbarian, found an inner principle of unity."[2] In fact, the liturgy was "the means by which the mind of the gentiles and the barbarians was attuned to a new view of life and a new concept of history."[3] "In the West," Dawson says, "after the fall of the Empire, the Church possessed in the liturgy a rich tradition of Christian culture as an order of worship, a structure of thought and a principle of life."[4] Accordingly, "The preservation and development of this liturgical tradition was one of the main preoccupations of the Church in the dark age that followed the barbarian conquest, since it was in this way that the vitality and continuity of the inner life of Christendom which was the seed of the new order were preserved."[5]

**Crisis of Culture**

In Dawson's view, this was an age of great liturgical creativity. The Christian cult operated to transfuse the existing barbarian traditions with a new ethical and spiritual quality. So impressive was this transfusion that, in Dawson's words, "It is almost impossible to convey to the modern mind the realism and objectivity with which the Christians of those ages viewed this liturgical participation in the mysteries of salvation."[6]

The dynamic relationship between liturgy and culture that Dawson saw operative in the formation of the Middle Ages inspired the beginning of the modern liturgical movement. The figure who stood at the head of this movement was Dom Prosper Guéranger, abbot of Solesmes from 1837 to 1875. Guéranger had long been considered an ultramontane reactionary intent on destroying the liturgical diversity of France in favor of the pure Roman rite. However, more recent scholarship has underlined Guéranger's importance in establishing a strong connection between liturgical renewal and the transformation of culture and society.

According to historian R. W. Franklin, one of the strengths in Guéranger's early work was the "vision of worship as a means to solve one of the great problems of the nineteenth century—the reintegration of matter and spirit."[7] Guéranger regarded the liturgy as "the instrument for an attack on the dissociation of the material and the spiritual in a predominately materialistic civilization which divided society into a secular sphere and an increasingly unimportant otherworldly spiritual sphere."[8] In a society torn apart by individualism, capitalism, and revolution, the liturgy would become, in Guéranger's vision, a force integrating individual and community, labor and spirituality, religion and life. The transcendent and inspiring character of worship and the intrinsic unifying power of Christian liturgy would reverse social disarray and restore the spirit of community characteristic of authentic Christian civilization.

Guéranger's dream was not, of course, realized, and the social effects of the early liturgical movement in France bear little positive comparison with the powerful influence of the liturgy in the formation of the early Middle Ages as identified by Dawson.

The same quality of vision, however, found expression in the early liturgical movement in the United States whose recognized leader was Father Virgil Michel, a monk at St. John's Abbey, Collegeville, Minnesota, until his death in 1938. Fr. Michel was an eloquent and prodigious exponent of the social power of the liturgy. Writing in *Orate Fratres* in 1935, Fr. Michel expressed his overwhelming conviction that the liturgy "is the one true basis of Christian culture and civilization."[9] The liturgy, he declared, "understood and lived after the mind of Christ and His Church—therefore lived both individually and socially—cannot but flower out into a genuine Christian culture that embraces every aspect of life and human experience."[10] Michel's conception of culture was inclusive. Culture, he said, "embraces all the activities and abilities of man, all the aspirations and inspirations of his nature, the entire field of human existence."[11] It includes individual and society, the intellectual and the material, belief and morality, art, custom, and law. For Michel, consequently, if the whole culture is to be changed and transformed, this can only be achieved by a vigorous living out of a true Christian spirit. For that reason, the living of the liturgical life must have as its aim "the penetration of all human contacts and activities with the spirit of Christ."[12] This recognition of the social power of the liturgy was, for Michel, "a most important truth for our day, when the Holy Father calls for a Christian reconstruction of the social order, when we are living in a world torn by a struggle of cultures, and when we are a minority group in a pagan, materialistic, and naturalistic culture and civilization, much as were the early Christians."[13] Accordingly, for Michel, there was an inner connection between the liturgical apostolate and Catholic social teaching.[14]

The question that may be asked in the light of this brief historical sketch is whether the liturgy of the post-conciliar Church has yielded the social and cultural transformation proclaimed in the modern liturgical movement and invoked by Dawson. The answer must, unfortunately, be a negative one. It is noteworthy that J. Bryan Hehir, the scholar most identified with the 1986 pastoral letter on Catholic social teaching and the U.S. economy entitled "Economic Justice for All," the controversial document of the National Conference of Catholic Bishops, is no less negative about the promised liturgical transformation of culture. Writing in 1980, Hehir concluded that "Fifteen years after the Council this potential remains largely unfulfilled in the Church in the United States."[15]

While there continues to be a great deal of energetic discussion

**Crisis of Culture**

today about the commitment to justice in the Church, this discussion does not appear to be matched by effective results. What is no less problematic is the fact that the vision of the social and cultural power of the liturgy analyzed by Dawson and embodied in the key figures of the modern liturgical movement no longer seems operative in discussions about justice and social transformation.

The impact of modern culture upon the perception and practice of the liturgy suggests some reasons for this decline of vision. I think that the fundamental reason why liturgy has lost a considerable part of its cultural and social power is related to the absorption into post-conciliar American Catholicism of profoundly negative dynamics operative in modern secular culture. Our appropriation of these dynamics has generated conceptions of liturgy that are destructive of and disorienting to liturgy's power to generate social and cultural change.

Each of three negative cultural dynamics that I shall identify and discuss—the subjectification of reality, the intimization of society, and the politicization of culture—contributes to cumulative liturgical dysfunction.

### THE SUBJECTIFICATION OF REALITY

The subjectification of reality is a pervasive social phenomenon about which a good deal has been written recently. The bestselling *Habits of the Heart* written by Robert Bellah and a team of social scientists documents the widespread assumption in modern American culture that the individual person rather than institutions or traditions is the center and origin of meaning and values. *Habits of the Heart* describes this view as "ontological individualism," the conviction that "the individual has a primary reality whereas society is a second-order, derived or artificial construct."[16]

Historian Christopher Lasch, following a similar thesis, has shown that the ontologization of individual experience is accompanied by a loss of confidence in history, future vision, politics, and social and cultural institutions.[17] For this reason, the structures and institutions that have traditionally embodied meaning and values lose their mediating power. The narcissistic individual created in the process becomes "the minimal self" existing in a survival state, shunning commitment to relationships and public life. As a result, personal energy is focused upon the relentless pursuit

**M. Francis Mannion**

4

of selfish needs, and the public world is scorned as meaningless and irrelevant.

There emerges what Lasch calls the "therapeutic sensibility" in which psychology and psychiatry replace the social institutions and modes that traditionally mediated personal growth and maturation.[18] In this climate, moral traditions and ethical systems survive only when appropriated into psychological and therapeutic modes for the articulation and expression of personal meaning and value. The idioms of therapy invade education, culture, and spirituality and undermine traditional, objective moral codes and systems.[19]

One of the consequences of subjectification and its attendant psychologization is the abandonment of the social and cultural arenas to consumerism and the propoganda of mass advertising. T. J. Jackson Lears has pointed out that "The decline of symbolic structures outside the self has been a central process in the development of a consumer culture joining advertising strategies and the therapeutic ethos."[20] In modern times, he says, "Advertisers began speaking to many of the same preoccupations addressed by liberal ministers, psychologists, and other therapeutic ideologues."[21] Lears characterizes the world in which we live as one in which the phenomenon of consumerism operates as a comprehensive cultural ideal, as a way of seeing wherein all significance evaporates from social institutions and a sense of trivialization and "weightlessness" prevails.

This process of trivialization is further compounded by the manner in which the electronic media reduce public life, education, art, and history to show business and entertainment. Institutions and ideas that have no direct therapeutic or consumer value are subject to appropriation by the entertainment media and lose thereby their moral seriousness and their integral value as autonomous agents of social edification.[22]

It is no secret that the subjectification of reality has had a profound effect upon the conceptions about and practice of religion in America. The authors of *Habits of the Heart* point out that the disposition to regard religion as a private matter has deep roots in the history of American individualism. The earlier tradition, however, assumed "a certain priority of the religious community over the individual."[23] More recently, that pattern has reversed, so that the majority of Americans now claim a personal rather than a social or ecclesiastical source for their religious beliefs. God is conceived rather as an "inner voice" than as the voice of community or tradition.

The modern subjectification of reality has its philosophical roots in the eighteenth-century Kantian "turn to the subject," and it finds contemporary expression in what theologian George Lindbeck describes as "experiential-expressive" modes of religion and religious reflection. According to Lindbeck, "The structures of modernity press individuals to meet God first in the depths of their souls and then, perhaps, if they find something personally congenial, to become part of a tradition or enter a church."[24] Religion, in this view, is a radically private and individual matter. Consequently, "Increasing numbers of people regard all religions as possible sources of symbols to be used eclectically in articulating, clarifying, and organizing the experiences of the inner self."[25] In line with this attitude are doctrines understood as "noninformative and nondiscursive symbols of inner feelings, attitudes, or existential orientations."[26]

Similarly, personal conscience is thought to determine authentic morality, with little reference to traditions of law or virtue. Alasdair MacIntyre has identified the problem of liberal ethics in an atomic view of individual existence in which personal will and feelings become the ultimate source of morality; "Everything may be criticized from whatever standpoint the self has adopted, including the self's choice of a standpoint to adopt."[27] MacIntyre characterizes this ethical position as emotivism, by which he means the view that the meaning of a moral judgment resides in the emotional quality of the individual response to an action or personal encounter. This generates the attitude, he says, that "Evaluative utterance can in the end have no point or use but the expression of my own feelings or attitudes and the transformation of the feelings and attitudes of others."[28]

The effects of subjectification upon the whole range of Christian institutions are devastating. The Bible, worship, preaching, ministry, doctrine, ecclesiastical structure, and communal life are thought useful to the extent that they serve the experience of inner truth and personal encounter with the divine. They become little more than functional guides for the discovery of inner realities and personal disposition.

There is ample evidence that subjectification of reality has be-

**M. Francis Mannion**

come systemic in American Catholicism since at least the late nineteen sixties and has found liturgical expression in what Nathan Mitchell has identified as a shift in the apprehension of the sacred. In Mitchell's words, the "sense of the sacred has moved, shifted its location,"[29] and has become progressively disengaged from its traditional location in the Church gathered at public worship. Now the sense of the sacred "is located 'inside,' in the personal history and geography of the self."[30] Consequently, "The sacred is closely attached to the self, not to rituals celebrated and shared in public."[31] As a result, modern Americans "look for the holy to reveal itself, not in the awe-inspiring rites of baptism and Eucharist, but in the awesome precincts of the self."[32]

In this movement, liturgy begins to be reconceived as a resource for getting in touch with the inward God or for celebrating inwardly constituted faith. The focus of engagement shifts from the transcendent God to the God apprehended in the mystery of the self. In this perspective, liturgy is understood to provide a nonintrusive space within which the Spirit may become operative in the heart and mind of the individual. Liturgy is regarded not as mediating divine presence, but as giving it shape and expression. Consequently, the real operations of worship are easily viewed as taking place outside formal liturgical contexts.

In this climate, the performance of liturgical rites takes on an experimental and improvisatory character. The search for liturgical expressions adequate to interior personal disposition, crisis, or need appears as a constant and intense preoccupation. The official and inherited liturgical forms tend to be regarded as of lesser value and are routinely replaced or supplemented by novel forms thought more authentic because they arise from the experience of individuals or groups in particular moments or situations.

The experiential-expressive framework imposed on liturgy as subjectification develops tends to recast evaluative criteria almost exclusively in terms of the inward needs of participants. Indeed, ritual forms will be evaluated so that what appears as therapeutically valuable will move into high relief while the more formal, complex, and ceremonial elements which mediate ecclesial significance will be reduced in importance.

If Lears and others are correct in seeing a connection between the therapeutic ethos and cultural consumerism, it should not be surprising that the subjectification of liturgical consciousness opens

**Crisis of Culture**

the way for poor and inappropriate artistic and communicative modes to enter the liturgy. Many commentators note a further consequence: the increasing appearance of a lack of dignity, seriousness, and reverence in liturgical celebration.

Those concerned about the subjectification of worship and liturgy believe that the process will reap a bitter harvest. As anthropologist Mary Douglas pointed out over a decade ago, the loss or rejection of ritual traditions ultimately involves the loss of the means by which religious conceptions and motivations are mediated and maintained. The collapse of ritual, according to Douglas, leads to the privatization of religious experience and finally to the reduction of the religious sense to humanistic philanthropy.[33] Without rite and tradition, Christians are bereft of the necessary language by which faith is formed and motivated. Without engagement with an objective liturgical system, the individual is cut off from the necessary sources of Christian existence. There is a loss of confidence not only in the Church and its rites and institutions, but ultimately in meaningful inner experience as the believer finds nothing "inside" and fades from faith in disillusionment.

Subjectification is, I believe, partly to blame for the profound disengagement of the liturgy from its traditional role in social and cultural transformation. With the pervasive tendency toward subjectification in the post-conciliar Church, there has emerged a massive loss of confidence in the social and cultural orders and, consequently, a loss of interest in and commitment to transforming them. If society and its institutions are regarded as irrelevant to authentic human existence, then the traditional role of the Church in transforming society is dismissed as romanticism or imperialism or, as we shall see later, collapses into political action. Because of the tendency to withdraw into individual subjectivity as the source of meaning and value, the liturgy is shorn of its traditional, sacramental formality and reconceived and practiced as therapy. In the process, the liturgy loses its power to embody a vision of social transformation, and its ability to elicit commitment to the social project is vitiated.


THE INTIMIZATION OF SOCIETY
The second pervasive dynamic with negative effects upon the liturgy and its role as transforming agent derives from what I call,

M. Francis Mannion

for want of a better expression, the intimization of society. This process is a logical outgrowth of the subjectification of reality and the attendant loss of confidence in social and cultural institutions. By the intimization of society, I mean the process by which social complexity is eschewed in favor of a model of human coexistence that puts ultimate value on bonds of intimacy, personal closeness, and radical familiarity.

In his classic study *The Fall of Public Man*, Richard Sennett has analyzed the modern collapse of the social in favor of the personal and the intimate. According to Sennett, "The reigning belief today is that closeness between persons is a moral good. The reigning aspiration today is to develop individual personality through experiences of closeness and warmth with others. The reigning myth today is that the evils of society can all be understood as evils of impersonality, alienation, and coldness."[34]

These convictions constitute what Sennett calls the "ideology of intimacy."[35] This ideology carries the pervasive conviction that "Social relationships of all kinds are real, believable, and authentic the closer they approach the inner psychological concerns of each person."[36] These convictions have their origin, according to Sennett, in narcissism—the cult of the self-obsessed personality— and destructive *gemeinschaft*, which had its origin in the dramatic emergence of personality into the public realm in the nineteenth century. In the intimate view of community which emerged at that time, the revelation of personality was thought to be an integral part of social interchange, and society itself began to be conceived of as a collective personality.[37] In this perspective, "All social phenomena, no matter how impersonal in structure, are converted into matters of personality in order to have meaning."[38] Indeed, society itself has meaning only to the extent that it is converted into "a grand psychic system."[39]

The most notable effect of the process of intimization is that people have come to expect psychological benefits throughout the whole range of human experience. As a result, they are unable to appreciate, as having any meaning, social elements and institutions that embody impersonality, public distance, and relational complexity. The public world seems to them empty and stale. Political life becomes a matter of formal obligation. Interchanges with strangers are looked upon as dry, formal, and unauthentic. Indeed, the stranger himself is regarded as threatening.[40]

**Crisis of Culture**

This whole process is accompanied by a commitment to social unmasking. As intimization advances, Sennet says that people "put pressure on each other to strip away the barriers of custom, manners, and gesture which stand in the way of frankness and mutual openness."[41] Diplomacy is thought to be incompatible with honesty, and reticence in self-revelation is regarded as a barrier to openness and real communication with others.

Intimization signifies for Sennett the end of public culture and of the codes of civility which allow for a wide variety of social relationships and the forging of bonds based on social distance.[42] Sennett complains that, unlike traditional societies, our culture today no longer has codes by which strangers recognize and greet each other in public. For that reason, public space is abandoned as "empty" and "dead."[43] Conventions which function as "rules for behavior at a distance from the immediate desires of the self" are abandoned.[44] Society and its institutions begin to be viewed as practical necessities rather than as expressions of an order of reality within which commitment is appropriate and has meaning.[45]

In the light of Sennett's analysis, it becomes clear why the rejection of systems of etiquette, protocol, and manners in our society represents more than a *dismissal* of the old-fashioned. Such rejection represents, rather, disillusionment with the complex nature of social existence. As a result, there occurs an unwitting loss of the ritual codes and systems that allow the negotiation of relations and commitments in the public world. All that remains are what Erving Goffman calls the "brief rituals" of interpersonal behavior and the "little pieties" exchanged between individuals.[46]

Like the subjectification of reality, the intimization of society has become operative at a profound level in American religion. The pervasiveness of convictions about the values of intimization in the religious sphere is documented by *Habits of the Heart*. The authors point out that the Church has come to be understood today primarily as a friendly gathering place for individuals who have experienced the divine or the holy in their personal lives. Typically, the Church is regarded as "an association of loving individuals" or "a community of empathic sharing."[47] It has become commonplace to think of the ultimate meaning and purpose of the Church in expressive-individualist terms. Thus it is commonly held that "Its value is as a loving community in which individuals can express the joy of belonging."[48]

**M. Francis Mannion**

10

The authors of *Habits of the Heart* indicate that this perspective is not uncommon among American Catholics, referring to the national study by Dean Hoge of The Catholic University of America which shows that the two values that American Catholics seek most are "personal and accessible priests" and "warmer, more personal parishes."[49]

Margaret O'Brien Steinfels has identified a significant strand in popular writing on the Church and ministry which is convinced that "The ideal structure is community; the ideal relationship, intimate; and the ideal size, small."[50] To people of these convictions, the larger Church appears cumbersome, unauthentic, and resistant to faith development. Ecclesial structures and operations are regarded as at best little more than functional resources.

In his recent book, *Redemptive Intimacy*, Dick Westley of Loyola University, Chicago, has proposed that the parish is a secondary community "whose major purpose is to offer programs and services."[51] For that reason, he says, the parish must be "built on *primary communities* where intimacy, interpersonal relations, and faith sharing can occur with regularity."[52] Westley proposes the highly problematic thesis that redemption is essentially a matter of intimacy. Indeed, he says, "Redemption is just another name for learning the lessons of intimacy."[53] The difficulty with this radical association of redemption and intimacy is the implication of the absence of redemptive mediation in the public, formal structures and operations of ecclesial life.

Sociologist Parker Palmer has pointed out that the kind of ecclesial coexistence which emerges from intimization both constricts ecclesial life and profoundly vitiates the church's public role. In his words, "When an idealized image of family is imposed upon the church, our experience in the congregation becomes constricted. . . . The church—where we might experience creative conflict, heterogeneity, and freedom for innovation—becomes dominated by the expectation of closeness and warmth."[54] In such a community, "People with whom we cannot achieve intimacy, or with whom we do not want to be intimate, are squeezed out."[55] The church easily becomes a preserve for persons of similar class and status. The strange is eliminated and the familiar is cultivated. Indeed, "Such a church can neither welcome the stranger nor allow the stranger in each of us to emerge."[56]

This constriction operates as a barrier to public life. The loss of

**Crisis of Culture**

confidence in the public, social arena and in the mediating power of ecclesiastical institutions leads to a loss of "a language genuinely able to mediate among self, society, the natural world, and ultimate reality."[57] Christians formed in this climate become singularly bereft of social literacy and of the means to understand and negotiate the relevance of Gospel values within the complexity of society. This evasion of the public world gives rise to what Richard Neuhaus calls "the naked public square," that is the public world sanitized of religious and moral values.[58] The church becomes a sect closed in upon itself, while the public world conducts its affairs impervious to religious and moral values.

The process of intimization is increasingly evident in popular conceptions and practices of the liturgy. In the light of social-scientific criticism, it is surprising that intimization is so widely and enthusiastically promoted at virtually every level of pastoral and liturgical renewal. Parker Palmer, in referring to the original definition of liturgy as a "public work," laments the fact that "The church in our time has lost the sense of public worship."[59] According to Nathan Mitchell, Christians today identify their deepest religious experiences "not with public ritual and worship, but with private, personal experiences of intimacy and relationship."[60] Indeed, he says, our primary model for the sacred today "is *intimacy, not liturgy.*"[61]

The pervasiveness of this shift accounts, in part, for the considerable emphasis today on the small group as the ideal configuration of the liturgical assembly. A high priority is placed on the promotion of intimacy, closeness, and familiarity in liturgical gatherings. The large, traditional congregation is rejected as anonymous and alienating, a barrier to authentic communal faith and worship.

In the shift toward intimacy, personality rather than rite tends to become the medium of liturgical communication and performance. Indeed, the personalities and charismatic qualities of clergy and liturgical ministers easily become the crucial factors of success in liturgical celebration. With this comes a rejection of the formal and the impersonal in liturgy and an amplification of the "little pieties" and "brief rituals"—to use Goffman's language—focused on moments of interpersonal sharing. Conventions of social distance are left behind in favor of the criteria of mutual intimacy. The ministry of hospitality is understood as creating friends and

**M. Francis Mannion**

intimates, rather than graceful and respectful interaction between the friends, fellow citizens, and strangers that make up the Christian body.[62]

In the process of intimization, liturgical rites and symbols lose the scale and complexity capable of engaging the Christian assembly with society, tradition, and history. As liturgy is conceptually repositioned within the configuration of intimate groups, it is shorn of broader cosmic symbolism and consequently loses its traditional spirit of grandeur, glory, and majesty. In effect, the journey into intimate community is a journey out of the public world.

As with the subjectification of reality, ecclesial appropriation of intimization distorts the power of the liturgy to transform society. In a Church where the process of intimization is advanced, social and ecclesial complexity is conceptually and practically rejected and that which is institutional experiences a loss of confidence. Consistent with this, the liturgy is tailored to the needs of intimate groups. It is shorn of public, social symbolism. Consequently, it no longer stands as a model of redeemed society and for that reason retains little ability to generate enthusiasm for social and cultural transformation.

### THE POLITICIZATION OF CULTURE

Let me turn finally to the politicization of culture. Raymond Williams' definition of culture introduces the issue here. Culture, according to Williams, "is the *signifying system* through which a social order is communicated, reproduced, experienced and explored."[63] This definition captures the nature of culture as the total complex of symbols and codes which penetrates every facet of human existence, generating common orientation, meaning, and commitment. Culture incorporates individual and society, nature and art, religion, morality, and history within an ordered, complex configuration of reality.

The politicization of culture, then, refers to the collapse of the multimodal processes and codes of culture into the single process of political activity. Though the politicization of life as a modern phenomenon is a complex matter and can be accounted for in a number of ways, it is clear that in North American and Western European societies it finds its systemic origins in the processes of

**Crisis of Culture**

subjectification and intimization and is essentially a liberal-capitalist phenomenon.

The politicization of culture and its relationship to the processes of subjectification and intimization can be set forth in the following way. In a world where these two latter processes are advanced, the public, institutional arena does not cease to exist when ignored or neglected. The complexity of life beyond the individual and the configuration of intimate groups does not disappear. Social complexity and public affairs continue to impinge upon the individual and to assert claims. Individuals are still forced to grapple with the larger, more complex world. This engagement, however, shorn of traditional modes, is reduced to the processes of working out legal and political conventions by which mutual respect for individual freedom, self-determination, and personal autonomy can be created and maintained. Consequently, the securing of freedom to pursue personal goals, to express oneself fully, and to secure a level of material well-being become the principal and virtually only public and social issues. In this way, society is reduced to a set of political and legal contracts into which individuals enter for the purpose of the autonomous advancement of individual interests.

Richard Neuhaus describes the process by which the politicization of public life is advanced. As religion and cultural values are relegated to the private realm, a public world devoid of moral and religious values is created which he calls the "naked public square." However, "When the value-bearing institutions of religion and culture are excluded, the value-laden concerns of human life flow back into the square under the banner of politics."[64] Though the relegation of religious and human values to the private sphere sterilizes public institutions of significance, the naked square "refuses to stay naked" and thus social meaning and values are politicized and culture is subsumed into the state. In this way, what Neuhaus calls "the pan-politicizing of life" is completed.[65]

Neuhaus identifies "the growing litigiousness of the American people" as a significant example of politicization.[66] By this he means that increasingly, conflicts in interpersonal relations find their way into the law courts. It is clear that recourse to litigation intensifies in proportion to the degree of breakdown of the conventions, formalities, and codes of civility that have traditionally

M. Francis Mannion

operated to resolve social conflict. The means for the working out of conflict and cooperation are becoming restricted to legal or political action.

Legal scholar Jethro Liebermann has analyzed similarly the manner in which appeal to the law courts has become a social epidemic.[67] Like Neuhaus, he is concerned that the traditional means of settling disputes have fallen away in favor of litigation. He argues that this litigiousness is essentially a social rather than a legal problem. "It is born of a breakdown in community, a breakdown that exacerbates and is exacerbated by the growth of law."[68] The courts have become the last repositories of social trust and will remain so, in Liebermann's view, until there is a restoration of trust in public institutions and a resurgence of commitment to social ethics.

This general process of politicization arises out of and intensifies the corruption and abandonment of the symbolic structures of culture, the "signifying systems" described by Raymond William. Educator Michael Warren speaks of "cultural pollution," by which he means "the despoiling of the chain, not of biogenerative processes, but of the processes of human signification, of human meaning."[69] Cultural pollution, he says, "proceeds to cause a breakdown of the processes of human valuing and understanding."[70] When cultural symbol systems collapse or become distorted, so too does the possibility of meaningful and civilized coexistence.

Another pair of educators, Denise and John Carmody, have spoken of a severe process of "deculturation" at work in the modern era.[71] They rightly observe that healthy societies have traditionally mustered and maintained social cohesiveness around a vital "cult," a vital set of symbols generating a deep veneration of life in all its expressions.[72] For that reason, the process of deculturation represents not only a loss of vital symbols, but a critical loss of transcendence and a collapse of the proper relationships between individual, nature, and society. "The result is that in our time the best and brightest have little support to dedicate themselves to art, genuine religion, scientific research, teaching, healing, parenting, or any of the other primary services of truth and human betterment."[73] In other words, "The movement toward transcendence having vacated the public scene, bad music, athletic displays, and a politics of power-plays command the center stage."[74] Essentially, this deculturation results in "a populace grown content with vulgarity."[75]

Whether we speak of cultural pollution despoiling the chain of signification or of deculturation leading to social vulgarity, the effect is the same: the arts, education, intellectual life, social and religious traditions, the discipline of family life, codes of civility and decorum, and the wise stewardship of creation survive as public and social matters only by reconstitution under the modes of politics and law.

The process of politicization has had a significant influence in the life of the Church in recent times and consequently has changed the contemporary conception and practice of the liturgy. Without doubt, the heightened concern for social justice and for Christian commitment to systemic social reform is one of the most remarkable elements to emerge from the renewal set in motion by the Second Vatican Council. The problem, however, appears in the post-conciliar trend—very advanced in some regions of the Church—to cast all social and cultural issues into political ones. This goes hand in hand with the abandonment of concerns for the organic transformation of society in a comprehensive and multimodal manner. The traditional methods of social transformation are laid aside in favor of narrower legal or political action. In the process, the theoretical complexity of social transformation is reduced to political concepts of social justice.

In a much-publicized lecture last year, theologian Avery Dulles argued for "the legitimacy of the Church's concern for social order while at the same time cautioning against the politicization of religion."[76] Dulles believes that while the Church has an inescapable mission to proclaim the reign of God, it must avoid doing so in a manner that ties the Gospel too closely to partisan or political agendas. Indeed, he says, "As a general rule, faithfulness to Jesus will incline the ecclesiastical authority to avoid entanglement in economic and political struggles."[77]

In similar vein, theologian J. Brian Benestad argues against the trend of collapsing the comprehensive, organic understanding of social justice into a narrow political scheme. He decries the fact that "The contemporary concern for social justice leads primarily to stress on public-policy initiatives, to a reorganization of the system, to social reform."[78] Accordingly, Benestad appeals to those elements of traditional Catholic social thought that focus on the

**M. Francis Mannion**

comprehensive transformation of society at all levels and through many non-political modes. Social justice, he says, focuses not only on the political and economic sectors of society but on the comprehensive common good of the whole society. For Benestad, then, the point of departure for social justice is primarily the action and commitment of virtuous and converted persons, not political action. For this reason, he is unhappy that today "The intellectual, moral and theological virtues are hardly mentioned in social-justice circles."[79] Regrettably, in his view, social justice as presently understood and promoted has little to do with virtuous action or with concepts of virtue that incline persons to fulfill duties toward society.

It becomes increasingly apparent that the dissociation of social transformation from traditional moral and cultural systems leads to frustration. As concepts of justice lose their concreteness and specificity and are disconnected from the integral elements of transformation embodied in the arts, education, family life, and in codes of personal and civic virtue, they become abstract and ideological. Theologian Wolfhart Pannenberg and moralist Stanley Hauerwas have identified, from different perspectives, the lack of reality and focus that attends the disconnection of the theory and practice of social justice from spirituality and the practice of virtue.[80] They show that purely political conceptions of the social order and of human commitment easily end in failure and frustration and cannot, given their abstract and unfocused character, yield a more just social order.

The politicization of ecclesial life is reflected in modern theories and practices of liturgy formed in political visions of human action and of the world in general. The effect of politicization is essentially one of narrowing and even overriding the intrinsic social vision of the liturgy itself and of redirecting its transforming power into political and legal channels. The process of politicization effects a kind of deculturation of the liturgy so that rites and symbols lose their power to generate social transformation according to their complex integral processes. Concern for the formation of personal virtue, civility, and intellect fades as the impetus for systemic political action assumes dominance in liturgical processes. Liturgical formation, conversion, and commitment are seen in activist terms rather than in terms of personal and communal holiness and sanctification. Concern for the poor and the oppressed is easily cast in the mold of political and legal reform.

When a left-wing ethos generated in radical or liberation movements becomes operative, the political edge becomes even more pronounced and generates a notably more intense character. In this framework, liturgy quickly assumes an attitude of protest and rage. The agendas advanced in this context habitually tend toward interest in the overthrow of unjust regimes, the restoration of human rights, the advancement of agrarian reform, or the rights of minorities.

Even the liturgy itself becomes the subject of ideological and politicized critiques. Where the Eucharist does not directly promote the cause of political liberation, it is prone to be regarded as in captivity to false powers.[81] The imposition of a feminist ideology will yield the view that "the Eucharist has become the ritual symbolization of the structural evil of sexism."[82]

The process of politicization, usually at work in much more subtle and diverse ways than I have outlined here, represents an inevitable manipulation of the liturgy. It is clear that such manipulation occurs when Christians "try to impose on the liturgy a social message it does not proclaim—even though, at the same time, they allow no sound of the liberating call proper to the liturgy."[83] This imposition overrides what Joseph Gelineau has called "the paschal dynamics of the Christian mystery."[84] By this, he means those dynamics flowing from Christ's death and resurrection that intend "the total transformation of relations between God, man and the cosmos."[85]

The appropriation of the dynamics of politicization into the liturgy represents another explanation of the inability of current liturgical practice to advance the ideal of social transformation promoted by the modern liturgical movement. It is clear that the phenomenon of politicization impoverishes human culture, distorts the Christian message, and severely restricts the ability of the liturgy to be an effective agent of social and cultural transformation.

This brings us back to our starting point in the social and cultural vision of the liturgy presented by Dawson, Gúeranger, and Michel. It is clear that their vision was cultural rather than political and recognized that the liturgy is effective as an agent of social transformation only when it generates intense commitment to

**M. Francis Mannion**

spirituality, art, education, intellectual life, the discipline of the Christian household, public virtue, and codes of civility. The perspective of these spiritual leaders makes it clear that the commitment to justice becomes effective only when generated and supported by a cultural rather than a political vision.

### THE WAY FORWARD

If the liturgy is to recover its power to transform the social and cultural environments, it will be necessary for the Church and those in positions of leadership and influence to confront the deleterious dynamics presently operative in much liturgical theology and practice. This cannot, of course, be a purely negative project. While we have been severely critical of the ecclesial and liturgical appropriations of current cultural attitudes identified in this essay, these influences should not be confused with some important features of the modern sensibility and of post-conciliar reform. Their positive features must be identified and appropriately incorporated into liturgical theory and practice.

While we must remain critical of the subjectification of reality, we cannot deny that the modern emphasis on subjectivity has had some positive benefits for the understanding and living of Christian faith. Many people have rightly pointed to a certain extrinsicism in pre-conciliar Roman Catholicism as a result of which faith and doctrine were inadequately related to human experience. The Second Vatican Council is correctly understood to have introduced a reversal of extrinsicism by emphasizing subjectivity in the renewal of doctrine, liturgy, and Christian life.

The fundamental problem, then, is not with a strong emphasis on subjectivity, but on subjectivity as the first principle of theological systems. We are not rejecting here the proper theological corrections that have been derived from modern phenomenologies of subjectivity but only the radical subjectification of reality that is widely pervasive in ecclesial and liturgical theory and practice today. We agree with Parker Palmer and the authors of *Habits of the Heart* that religious inwardness and subjectivity are not to be rejected but rather disciplined and reconnected to the public, institutional realm.[86] In the area of liturgy, this means not a rejection of concerns for subjective experience and interiority but a conceptual and practical restoration of the liturgy as the origin and context of authentic subjectivity and spirituality.[87]

**Crisis of Culture**

The emphasis on community and on active participation are indisputably valid features of conciliar and post-conciliar liturgical reform. The development and promotion of prayer meetings, spiritual support groups, and the advancement of faith through small gatherings have well-documented value in pastoral renewal.

The problem is not essentially in the search for an experience of the Church that is hospitable, involving, and supportive, but in the tendency to make intimacy the principal element of authentic Christian community with the result that the public, formal, and institutional elements of the Church are rejected as meaningless and inauthentic. The challenge, then, is to incorporate pastoral possibilities for hospitality and for mutual engagement and support into parish and ecclesiastical communities without generating the ideology of intimacy and its anti-institutional consequences. The choice is not between models of radical intimacy and inhospitality and alienation. Parker Palmer describes the proper attitude when he suggests the paradox that the Church must be "a company of strangers." The Church must create communities, he says, "which are not mere extensions of private security, but which bridge the private and the public, leading us from the familiarities of private life into the strangeness of the public realm."[88] While the Church does not disavow the values of intimacy, it does recognize that the only authentic intimacy is with and through God, for "in the spacious hospitality of God's love, the Christian can become 'intimate' even with people seen once, or not at all."[89]

Given the importance of images and metaphors in shaping and orienting faith, the image of the Church as city seems, in the present context, more adequate than the images of Church as family or community of friends. Indeed, only when conceived as a city rather than as an intimate community can the vocation of the Church to possess and redeem all the dimensions of social reality emerge into proper relief. Only in a Church truly public and publicly concerned will the liturgy be able to speak to and generate commitment to the transformation of the social and cultural environments.[90]

The politicization of the Gospel is not the same thing as genuine Christian commitment to service of the poor and the oppressed. The 1971 Synod of Bishops made the depth of the latter commitment clear when it declared that "Action on behalf of justice and participation in the transformation of the world fully appear to us as a constitutive dimension of the preaching of the Gospel, or, in other words, of the Church's mission for the redemption of the human race and its liberation from every oppressive situation."[91] Undoubtedly, Christians have in the past often failed to carry out this commitment to systemic and structural reform. For that reason, the occasional need for this kind of reform is properly recognized today. Nevertheless, the systemic and political cannot become the principal or exclusive focus of social transformation.

The essential objection, then, to the politicization of the Church's social mission is that it narrows the scope of this mission, robs it of the richness of vision that emerges from an organic conception of society, and effectively restricts its work of transformation to a very few. In contrast, the vision of the Church's social mission embodied in the liturgy itself generates concern for the transformation of the total human city. It inspires political action in the most profound sense of serving and preparing the way for the heavenly city, the New Jerusalem.[92] The kind of commitment that emerges from this total view is shot through with an ethos of praise, thanksgiving, and sacrifice and remains fundamentally subject to the power of Christ risen and exalted.[93] The rich and diverse symbolic operations of the liturgy point Christians to the great variety of ways by which the transformation of society and human culture can be achieved. They provide the energy for transformation within the diverse orders of individual existence, household and community, city and nation. Most of all, the liturgy directs Christians not to grand political schemes but to virtuous action, to the recognition proposed by Stanley Hauerwas that "Justice often demands no more than the most common acts of care."[94]

## NOTES

1. Christopher Dawson, *Religion and the Rise of Western Culture* (Garden City, N.Y.: Image Books, 1958) 26 ff.
2. *Ibid.* 41.
3. *Ibid.*
4. *Ibid.* 43.
5. *Ibid.*

6. *Ibid.* 42. See also the chapter entitled "The Influence of Liturgy and Theology on the Development of Byzantine Culture" in Christopher Dawson, *The Formation of Christendom* (New York: Sheed and Ward, 1967) 136–153.

7. R. W. Franklin, "The Nineteenth Century Liturgical Movement," *Worship* 53 (1979) 25.

8. *Ibid.* 25–26. See also R. W. Franklin, "Guéranger: A View on the Centenary of His Death," *Worship* 49 (1975) 318–328; "Guéranger and Pastoral Liturgy: A Nineteenth-Century Context," *Worship* 50 (1976) 146–162; "Guéranger and Variety in Unity," *Worship* 51 (1977) 378–399; "Response: Humanism and Transcendence in the Nineteenth Century Liturgical Movement," *Worship* 59 (1985) 342–353.

9. Virgil Michel, "Nine Years After," *Orate Fratres* 10 (1935–36) 5.

10. *Ibid.*

11. Virgil Michel, "Liturgy and Catholic Life," 193 (unpublished manuscript), quoted in Paul B. Marx, *Virgil Michel and the Liturgical Movement* (Collegeville: The Liturgical Press, 1957) 257.

12. Michel, "Nine Years After," 6.

13. *Ibid.* 5.

14. H. A. Reinhold commented that "For Virgil Michel the labor encyclicals of Leo XIII and the liturgical reforms of Pius X did not just by accident happen within one generation, but were responses to cries of the masses for Christ, who had power and gave the good tidings. They belonged together." H. A. Reinhold, "The Liturgical Movement to Date," *National Liturgical Week—1947*, 11. Michel was careful to point out, however, that "The liturgy does not offer a detailed scheme of economic reconstruction, or anything of the kind. But it does give us a proper concept and understanding of what society is like, through its model, the Mystical Body." Letter to Martin Schirber, O.S.B., November 27, 1935, quoted in Marx, *Virgil Michel and the Liturgical Movement*, 205. See also *The Social Question: Essays on Capitalism and Christianity by Father Virgil Michel*, O.S.B. Selected and edited by Robert L. Spaeth (Collegeville: Office of Academic Affairs, St. John's University, 1987).

15. J. Bryan Hehir, foreword to *Liturgy and Social Justice*, ed. Mark Searle (Collegeville: The Liturgical Press, 1980) 10.

16. Robert N. Bellah et al., *Habits of the Heart: Individualism and Commitment in American Life* (New York: Harper and Row, 1985) 334.

17. Christopher Lasch, *The Culture of Narcissism: American Life in An Age of Diminishing Expectations* (New York: Warner Books 1979); also *The*

**M. Francis Mannion**

*Minimal Self: Psychic Survival in Troubled Times* (New York: W. W. Norton, 1984).

18. Lasch, *The Culture of Narcissism*, 33.

19. See Philip Rieff, *The Triumph of the Therapeutic: Uses of Faith After Freud* (New York: Harper and Row, 1966). Rieff elsewhere comments about the manner in which the hospital has, in our time, come to fulfill the social role formerly played by the church or the cathedral. See *Freud: The Mind of the Moralist* (Garden City, N.Y.: Doubleday 1961) 390.

20. T. J. Jackson Lears, "From Salvation to Self-Realization: Advertizing and the Therapeutic Roots of the Consumer Culture, 1880–1930," in *The Culture of Consumption: Critical Essays in American History, 1880–1980*, ed. Richard Wightman Fox and T. J. Jackson Lears (New York: Pantheon Books, 1983) 21.

21. *Ibid.* 4.

22. See Neil Postman, *Amusing Ourselves to Death: Public Discourse in the Age of Show Business* (New York: Viking Penguin, 1985).

23. *Habits of the Heart*, 227.

24. George A. Lindbeck, *The Nature of Doctrine: Religion and Theology in a Postliberal Age* (Philadelphia: The Westminster Press, 1984) 22.

25. *Ibid.*

26. *Ibid.* 16.

27. Alasdair MacIntyre, *After Virtue: A Study in Moral Theory*, 2nd ed. (Notre Dame: University of Notre Dame Press, 1984) 31.

28. *Ibid.* 24.

29. Nathan Mitchell, "The Sense of the Sacred," in *Parish: A Place for Worship*, ed. Mark Searle (Collegeville: The Liturgical Press, 1981) 74.

30. *Ibid.* 72.

31. *Ibid.* 69.

32. *Ibid.* 71.

33. Mary Douglas, *Natural Symbols: Explorations in Cosmology* (London: Pelican Books, 1973) 19 ff.

34. Richard Sennett, *The Fall of Public Man* (New York: Alfred A. Knopf, 1977) 259.

35. *Ibid.*

36. *Ibid.*

37. *Ibid.* 219 ff.

38. *Ibid.* 219.

39. *Ibid.* 4.

**Crisis of Culture**

40. *Ibid.* 3 ff.

41. *Ibid.* 338.

42. *Ibid.* 259 ff.

43. *Ibid.* 12.

44. *Ibid.* 266.

45. *Ibid.* 263. The effects of this process upon family life are analyzed in Christopher Lasch, *Haven in a Heartless World: The Family Besieged* (New York: Basic Books, 1977).

46. Erving Goffman, *Relations in Public* (New York: Harper and Row, 1971) 63.

47. Bellah, *Habits of the Heart,* 228.

48. *Ibid.* 230.

49. *Ibid.* 232. See Dean R. Hoge, *Converts, Dropouts, Returnees: A Study of Religious Change Among Catholics* (Washington: United States Catholic Conference; New York: Pilgrim Press, 1981) 167.

50. Margaret O'Brien Steinfels, "The Laity: Not of One Mind," *Church* 3 (Fall 1987) 52.

51. Dick Westley, *Redemptive Intimacy: A New Perspective for the Journey to Adult Faith* (Mystic, Ct.: Twenty-third Publications, 1981) 140.

52. *Ibid.* Emphasis in original.

53. *Ibid.* 103.

54. Parker J. Palmer, *The Company of Strangers: Christians and the Renewal of America's Public Life* (New York: Crossroads, 1983) 120.

55. *Ibid.*

56. *Ibid.* The comment of the authors of *Habits of the Heart* on the superficial quality of intimization is instructive. The need for personal intimacy, they say, "suggests why the local church, like so many other voluntary communities, indeed like the contemporary family, is so fragile, requires so much energy to keep it going, and has so faint a hold on commitment when such needs are not met." (232).

57. Bellah, *Habits of the Heart,* 237.

58. Richard John Neuhaus, *The Naked Public Square: Religion and Democracy in America* (Grand Rapids: William B. Eerdmans Publishing Company, 1984).

59. Palmer, *The Company of Stangers,* 136.

60. Mitchell, "The Sense of the Sacred," 71.

61. *Ibid.* Emphasis in original.

## M. Francis Mannion

62. On this, see Robert E. Meagher, "Strangers at the Gates: Ancient Rites of Hospitality," *Parabola* 2:4 (1977) 10–15.

63. Raymond Williams, *The Sociology of Culture* (New York: Schocken Books, 1982) 13. Emphasis in original.

64. Neuhaus, *The Naked Public Square*, 159.

65. *Ibid.* 158.

66. *Ibid.* 157.

67. Jethro K. Liebermann, *The Litigious Society* (New York: Basic Books, 1983).

68. *Ibid.* 186.

69. Michael Warren, "Catechesis and the Problem of 'Popular' Culture," *The Living Light* 23 (1987) 133.

70. *Ibid.*

71. Denise Lardner Carmody and John Tully Carmody, "Vogelin and the Restoration of Order: A Meditation," *Horizons* 14:1 (1987) 82–96.

72. *Ibid.* 82–83.

73. *Ibid.* 84.

74. *Ibid.*

75. *Ibid.*

76. Avery Dulles, "The Gospel, The Church and Politics," *Origins* 16 (1987) 637.

77. *Ibid.* 646.

78. J. Brian Benestad, "The Catholic Concept of Social Justice: A Historical Perspective," *Communio* 11 (1984) 364.

79. *Ibid.*

80. See the chapter entitled "Sanctification and Politics" in Wolfhart Pannenberg, *Christian Spirituality* (Philadelphia: The Westminster Press, 1983) 50–70. For a summary of the views of Hauerwas on this matter, see his essay "Should Christians Talk So Much About Justice?" *Books and Religion* 14:5/6 (1986) 5, 14–15.

81. This is the thesis of Tissa Balasuriya, *The Eucharist and Human Liberation* (Maryknoll: Orbis Books, 1979).

82. Elisabeth Schüssler Fiorenza, "Tablesharing and the Celebration of the Eucharist," in *Can We Always Celebrate the Eucharist?* (Concilium 152), ed. Mary Collins and David Power (New York: The Seabury Press/Edinburgh: T. and T. Clark Ltd., 1982) 4. Though we cannot go into it here, it is noteworthy that liberation and feminist theologies have their roots in systems other than liberalism and, therefore, the

kind of politicization they represent is related only indirectly to the processes of subjectification and intimization.

83. P. de Béthunes, quoted in Joseph Gelineau, "Celebrating the Paschal Liberation," in *Politics and Liturgy* (Concilium 92), ed. Herman Schmidt and David Power (New York: Herder and Herder, 1974), 111.

84. Gelineau, "Celebrating the Paschal Liberation," 111.

85. *Ibid.* 113.

86. Bellah, *Habits of the Heart*, 163, 248; Palmer, *The Company of Strangers*, 155.

87. For a similar suggestion, see Carol Doran and Thomas H. Troeger, "Reclaiming the Corporate Self: The Meaning and Ministry of Worship In a Privatistic Culture," *Worship* 60 (1986), 200–210.

88. Palmer, *The Company of Strangers*, 121.

89. *Ibid.* 110.

90. See the chapter entitled "The City" in Urban Holmes T. Holmes III, *Ministry and Imagination* (New York: The Seabury Press 1976), 13–34; also Aidan Kavanagh, *On Liturgical Theology* (New York: Pueblo Publishing Company, 1984), especially the chapter entitled "The Church," 39–51.

91. Introduction, *Justice in the World*. Text in *Justice in the Marketplace. Collected Statements of the Vatican and the United States Catholic Bishops on Economic Policy, 1891–1984* (Washington: United States Catholic Conference, 1985) 250.

92. See Herman Schmidt, "Lines of Political Action and Contemporary Liturgy," in *Politics and Liturgy* (Concilium 92) 13–33.

93. On this see the chapter entitled "Ethics" in Geoffrey Wainwright, *Doxology: The Praise of God in Worship, Doctrine, and Life* (New York: Oxford University Press, 1980) 399–434; also Mark Searle, "Serving the Lord with Justice," in *Liturgy and Social Justice*, 13–35.

94. Hauerwas, "Should Christians Talk So Much About Justice?" 14.

**M. Francis Mannion**

Mark Searle

# Private Religion, Individualistic Society, and Common Worship

INTRODUCTION

It is, on the face of it, rather odd that twenty-five years after the promulgation of the Liturgy Constitution we should still be worrying about how to form worshipping communities. The reformed rites and concomitant "programs of instruction" (SC, #14) were supposed to cultivate the kind of active participation which would of itself engender a sense of the Church at prayer. However, as we now see more clearly, the worship community is formed not only by liturgy and catechesis, but by the larger culture in which its members live and work. In a sense, this makes talk about adapting the liturgy to our culture somewhat otiose: while we have been talking, adaptation has been happening anyway. It might not be too much of an exaggeration to say that the major transformations occurring in our liturgical practice have occurred not as a result of deliberate decision, but by casual contagion and incorporation.[1]

We tend to think too much of what the Church might bring to society and too little of what society is already bringing to the Church. We enthuse about what new prayers and new liturgical music might to do shape the liturgical assembly, overlooking the fact that culture has gotten there before us, unconsciously shaping the attitudes and language of both the experts and the participants. While this paper cannot claim to offer anything very original, it will have served its purpose if it brings to the attention of those responsible for liturgy some of the findings of those whose task in life it is to study our culture. We shall begin by identifying some of the chief characteristics of our culture, particularly as they affect religiosity in our society; then, we shall look for indications of the influence of these cultural traits in our liturgical practice. Finally, I will offer some tentative suggestions about the possibility of genuinely public worship in America.

## I. CULTURE

As I have already suggested, one of the problems faced by those of us whose preoccupations center on the parish and its liturgy is the tendency to become narrowly parochial in outlook. All too rarely do we consider the wider world in which the parish is situated or become actively engaged in issues affecting the broader life of the community. We have, many of us, little sense of what the liturgy looks like to parishioners who come from that larger world or of how limited a role religion can play in their larger lives. This same innocence of the society in which Christians actually live characterizes much writing on liturgy, not least the Liturgy Constitution itself. Paragraphs 41 and 42 of the Constitution, in describing the life of the diocese as centered around the bishop presiding in his cathedral—and in only acknowledging as an afterthought that the bishop cannot be everywhere, so that we have to have parishes led by priests—seem to hearken back to the simpler days of late antiquity when, though the reality rarely matched the ideal, one bishop presided over one Eucharist celebrated by an undivided community in a small Mediterranean town.

There is more than a hint of nostalgia here which feeds into our modern hunger for community. British sociologist Bryan Wilson, with a foreigner's critical eye, picks up the way American churches attempt to bring a sense of old-fashioned community to modern life:

> The Church . . . represents the values of the agrarian or communal preindustrial society: its forms are moulded from that stage of social development and it participates in the warmth, stability and fundamental mutual involvements of a type of community life. That this community is, in the nature of American society, not so much a fossil as a reproduction piece, is less damaging in the eyes of those who have little experience of community life than in the eyes of visiting Europeans. The synthetic nature of the community-orientation of many American churches is evident to those from more traditional cultures; the personalized gestures of the impersonal society acquire an almost macabre quality for those who have experienced the natural, spontaneous operation of rural community life. . . . And yet it seems evident, whether the Church does fulfil functions of this kind or not, men obviously get some, perhaps purely sentimental, satisfactions from presuming that it does.[2]

If Wilson is right, much of our talk about the worship community is really self-delusion. We yearn for the homely togetherness

**Mark Searle**

and directness of an earlier and simpler age, but our attempts to restore it merely parody it. Behind the cheery informality of our celebrations and our "ministers of hospitality," the profoundly impersonal quality of our interactions remains untouched. To get some idea of why this might be the case, we need to look at some of the distinguishing characteristics of modern American life. Here I have to reproduce in broad strokes the more nuanced findings of a number of sociologists and to risk the appearance of describing a universal state of affairs when I am only trying to single out some particular tendencies selected for the corrosive effect they can have on communal religious identity.

1. *Religious Privatism.* For over 1500 years, European Christianity experienced a form of social life in which Church and state were united and in which religious uniformity was the safeguard of social coherence. But the United States has never known this experience. It was founded by dissenters, recusants, and nonconformists looking for precisely the space to live out their religious convictions that they could not find in Europe. Deliberately repudiating the establishment of a single state Church, America self-consciously nurtured religious tolerance which meant accepting religious pluralism—not one Church binding the nation together in a single religious community but a growing multiplicity of churches and sects offering every citizen the freedom to worship in accordance with his or her conscience.

The benefits of such an arrangement we have long since learned to take for granted, but it has also had consequences for religion which we often overlook. It has essentially privatized religion in this country, and in two senses.

In the first place, religion is privatized for the individual. Freedom to practice religion in accordance with one's conscience also implies freedom to choose which religion, if any, one will practice. It devolves into a matter of purely personal preference. "My religious beliefs are my own business and nobody else's."

Second, privatization affects the denominations themselves since they have no public role to play and no official standing. They are demoted to secondary institutions caring for the needs of private individuals. In the eyes of the state, all religions are equally good and equally useful, and all are equally banned both from direct intervention in affairs of state and from access to the state educational system. Their place is in the domestic and private sphere where they may seek to motivate and guide individual citizens, but there the line is drawn.

Because religion is relegated to the private sphere and because religious affiliation is purely a matter of personal choice, the churches find themselves in competition with one another for members. Having lost the power to compel a following, their moral authority undermined by the very variety of religious brands on the market, they are reduced to peddling religion as something that meets people's personal needs. The image of religion as a market is one that recurs in writings about religion in America. So David Martin writes:

> The clergy are assimilated to the role of rival entrepreneurs running varied religious services on a mixed laissez-faire and oligopolistic basis. . . . Religious styles constantly adapt and accept vulgarization in accordance with the stylistic tendencies of their varied markets . . .[3]

Martin Marty, an astute observer of American religion, confirms this point:

> "The drift of religion today is, if anything, moving towards an utterly free market in which little trace of fate, election, or predestination remains."[4]

The result is a tendency for Americans to belong to churches, but on their own terms. They come, not to submit to historical tradition and religious discipline in response to God's call, but for their own personal reasons and to meet their own personal needs.

This drift towards privatism and subjectivism in religion is not merely the result of religious pluralism. It is a religious symptom of a larger upheaval in social life which we might call "massification."

2. *Massification*. The term "massification" is intended to identify a stage in the evolution of a society where the different social institutions have become so specialized and the ordering of society so complex that the democratic process can no longer work effectively. Instead, basic decisions affecting the life of the people are made by technocrats, and most of the population, losing perspective and control, are "maneuvered by the mass media to the point where they believe nothing they have not heard on the radio,

**Mark Searle**

seen on television, or read in the newspapers."[5] As the fate of our lives rests in the hands of fewer and fewer people further and further away, we are rendered powerless in our own society, incapable of engaging effectively in the direction of its processes. We are, as Karl Marx would say, "alienated."

Marx, of course, analyzed the problems of alienation in the wake of the nineteenth-century industrial revolution in which the advent of machinery dramatically altered the patterns of labor and made mass production possible. Society suffered the mass displacement of workers from the rural areas into the new towns, people uprooted from their traditional communities and reduced to the status of units of production. Yet, as sociologist David Martin has pointed out, this first industrial revolution left intact many of the characteristic features of the pre-industrial world: the small business, the family farm, personal contact between masters and servants, a "respectable" working class. Many of the traditional forms of social relations continued to exist, and where they did, religion held its own.

It was the advent of the second industrial revolution, that of the twentieth century, argues Martin, that led to the further and almost complete disintegration of social bonds. Ironically, this second revolution was essentially a revolution in the means of communication: the development of the telephone, of radio and television; the replacement of the railroads by the interstate highways, of ships by air transportation. The new communications media have finally swept away the remnants of the older forms of community.

> The institutions congruent with modern industry, with bureaucracy and technical rationality, are large, impersonal, and mechanical in their operation. The intimate bonds of horizontal community, working-class or otherwise, are broken up; the ecology of the city encourages fragmentation; the small shop gives way to the supermarket; the family firm enters the international consortium; the small farm is rationalized into larger units run by scientific agriculture; the moderate-sized office is swallowed up in large-scale bureaucracy; the community of school is wrecked by education factories operated by mobile teachers.[6]

Not every American, of course, is affected by these changes to the same degree, but these new developments set a style of life, establish expectations, and engender attitudes and values very different from those of the world we have now lost. Most generally and most importantly, the premium placed on cost-efficiency and profitability, on functional specialization and expertise creates a society where the dominant values are functional values and where matters of "ultimate concern" are relegated to the private realm. Since religion is about matters of "ultimate concern," it finds no place in public life, being left for each individual to decide for himself.

The effect, then, of massification is to reinforce the effects of pluralism, making the individual the sole arbiter of ultimate values and thereby undermining the bonds that create genuine community. What holds us together as a society is not, as in most societies, a common world view, a "sacred cosmos,"[7] but the patterns of production and consumption into which we are socialized by secular education and the seductions of the mass media.

3. *Individualism.* The wondrous capacity of human beings to adapt to their environment is strikingly displayed in the manner in which modern people have come to terms with the split between public and private selves and with the removal of questions of ultimate concern from the public to the private forum. Radical individualism is an outlook on life which results from making a virtue of necessity and turning the loss of community into a gain for the self. Radical individualism celebrates the freedom that is now ours to select our own values and priorities without reference to any wider framework of common purpose or beliefs. In the words of Robert Bellah:

> We believe in the dignity, indeed the sacredness, of the individual.
> Anything that would violate our right to think for ourselves, make
> our own decisions, live our lives as we see fit, is not only morally
> wrong, it is sacrilegious.[8]

With the supports, the constraints, and the commitment required by genuine community removed, we are free to pursue the good as we see it. Bellah says:

> What is good is what one finds rewarding. If one's preferences
> change, so does the nature of the good. Even the deepest ethical
> values are justified as matters of personal preference. Indeed, the
> ultimate ethical rule is that individuals should be able to pursue
> whatever they find rewarding, constrained only by the requirement
> that that not interfere with the "value systems" of others.[9]

**Mark Searle**

So much do we take the autonomy of the individual for granted that it is difficult to get a clear perspective on this radical individualism. It is hard to observe when it is itself the lens through which we observe all else. Nonetheless, its characteristics would include the following:

- a proclivity for seeing the individual as prior to society and thus for seeing society—and the Church—as a conglomeration of autonomous individuals rather than seeing them as products of an historical community;
- a tendency to prefer one's own judgment over the judgment of tradition or authority, a tendency which, paradoxically, also tends to make for uncritical conformism since one tends to look to others to confirm one's own opinion and to seek out the company of like-minded people;
- a preference for "gut feelings" and emotional spontaneity over the arduous task of rational argument, for following one's feelings rather than thinking things through; thus public debate declines into sloganeering and elections into popular contests and public decision-making into a contest between pressure groups;
- the intrinsic value of work and service is overlooked and replaced by a quest for self-realization or, where that fails, by the pursuit of greater income;
- the freedom to make personal decisions is gained at the expense of turning over public decisions to managers and technocrats: in other words, the expanded opportunities for personal freedom occur at the expense of our involvement in the public life of our society.[10]

All this flows from the nature of modern individualism: the assertion of self-interest at the expense of public interest, the claim of the self to be the final arbiter of ultimate values, the abdication of responsibility for one another and for society in the belief that each of us is finally only answerable to ourselves.

The effects of such radical individualism, where it prevails, is a radical incapacity for community. In an older understanding of society, Philip Rieff points out, "The sense of well-being of the individual was dependent upon his full, participant membership in a community." This is still the vision upheld by the Church and her liturgy, we might note. But to the degree that communitarian values are subordinated to the ultimate conviction that people "must free themselves from binding attachments to communal purposes in order to express more freely their individualities,"[11]

**Private Religion, Individualistic Society, Common Worship**

our attempts at fostering a sense of community in our liturgies will remain exercises in self-delusion. For clearly we have not given up on community altogether: indeed, some parishes talk of little else. But to the extent that we seek community as a means of self-fulfillment, looking to it to meet our needs but reluctant to submit ourselves to its constraints, we merely succeed in turning our parish liturgies into "life-style enclaves," as Bellah calls them,[12] the coming-together of people who enjoy the same things. Since such a coming-together is predicated only on the overlapping of particular tastes and interests, it can never engage the whole person and will only continue to be frequented as long as those tastes continue to be satisfied and those interests met.

4. *Civil Religion.* Despite all that has been said, it would be a mistake to suppose that, because religion has been rendered a matter of personal predilection and because the churches no longer have a public role, there is no place for religion in public life. On the contrary, what Robert Bellah, following Rousseau, has called "civil religion" has a significant role in our national life.[13] The Pledge of Allegiance speaks of our being "one nation under God," while the name of God is quite regularly invoked in public discourse. But this American God is not to be confused with the God of the Jews and Christians and is never trinitarian. Martin Marty calls it "the God of Religion-in-General, a harmless little divinity who has nothing in common with the God of Christianity."[14] While Bellah argues the positive value of civil religion—its subordination of the will of the people to a transcendent sacred, its ability to build up national solidarity or to evoke personal motivation for national goals—it is also important to recognize that it constitutes a sort of national pan-religiosity which coopts and assimilates to itself the specific beliefs and value-systems of historical Christian churches. To the degree that it succeeds, church-going Americans fail to discriminate between the religion of nationalism and the Christianity they profess. All become jumbled up together, thereby depriving Christian communities of the distance they need to distinguish between historical Christianity and contemporary American culture. They lose their critical and prophetic voice, serving only to affirm the cultural values we have been discussing. Instead of being resources for the recovery of genuine community, the churches and their liturgies end up ped-

**Mark Searle**

dling "synthetic" community, designed to accommodate people's longing for community but finally incapable of actually engendering community.

Religious privatism and massification, radical individualism and civil religion are the divisive forces with which liturgy and catechesis must contend if a genuine community of worship is to be built up. They are all the more powerful and pervasive because they are not the subject of conscious reflection in most parishes. We go with these forces because we know no other way, so that even the communitarian language and practices of our tradition are reinterpreted, quite unconsciously, to conform to our cultural expectations.

## II. CULT

We need hardly wait, then, for some national commission to undertake the work of cultural adaptation of the liturgy in this country since it is already well under way. Our parishes and our parish liturgies reflect our times as much as they harbor memories of time past and proclaim a vision of time to come. David Martin, an English sociologist of religion, reflecting on the pressures of modernity, gives some clues about where to look for symptoms of acculturation:

> The Church itself must reflect these varied pressures: the bureaucratization and impersonality, and the reaction in the form either of a familistic suburban religion or else in radical celebrations of personal authenticity or community. The rationalization of church organizations and liturgy proceeds *pari passu* with cults of encounter, authenticity and religious excitement, all of which leap over the constricting limits of the contemporary organization of role.[15]

Martin is suggesting that church life in general and liturgy in particular will vacillate between, on the one hand, reflecting the anonymity and bureaucratization of society and, on the other, manifesting signs of reaction against the conditions of contemporary life either in the pseudo-family atmosphere cultivated by suburban fellowshipping or in the more intensive emotional atmosphere of renewal groups.

The first pole is familiar enough: the large, anonymous parishes where one can go for years without knowing more than a handful of people by name; the congregation where, week by week, most people seem to be from out of town; the Saturday evening Masses

**Private Religion, Individualistic Society, Common Worship**

in half-empty churches where elderly Catholics accompany the hurried mutter of the Mass with the flutter of missalettes and the reluctant singing of an opening and closing hymn before hurrying home to lock their doors and settle down to an evening of television. In short, those liturgies we commonly assert to be "dead" merely reflect the life of our times: anonymous, private, functional, and individualistic.

The second pole, on the other hand, is represented by what usually passes for "good liturgy": the smoothly orchestrated celebrations of suburbia with their choirs and folk-groups, their "easy-listening" music, their firm handshakes, and their abundance of lay ministers in bright dresses and sharp suits. But for more radical reactions against the anonymity and impersonalism of our society, we should probably look outside the usual parish setting to Masses celebrated on the living-room floor in religious houses where "Father Mike" wears a stole and all join hands as he improves on the Eucharistic traditions of centuries with a sizeable dose of earnest informality; or we might look to youth Masses where the Gospel is reduced to God wanting us to be ourselves, and the last vestiges of ritual formality yield before a burning desire for authenticity. Better still, look to the culminating liturgy at experiences of encounter and renewal where deep and extensive sharing over twenty-four hours reaches climax and consummation in a "meaningful worship experience" oblivious both to history and to the future, celebrating the "now."

Robert Bocock, in his *Ritual in Industrial Society*, argues that ritual survives into the modern era but with quite a different role from that which it exercised in earlier times. In societies simpler and more homogeneous than our own, fixed rituals gave expression to a collective consciousness shared by all members of society, thereby enabling individuals to find themselves in a communitarian context. In industrial society, however, what collective consciousness there *is* is the product of the processes of production and consumption. Some ritual actions, like the rites of civil religion—including going to church—still serve to foster a shared world view and catch us up and identify us with the larger society, but, says Bocock:

> at the level of total society this is rarely the case. Rituals can be used in modern society for coming to know ourselves as individuals, as our own center of action. "The individual feels himself less

acted upon; he becomes more a source of spontaneous activity. . . .
It is still from society that [ritual] takes all its forces, but it is not to
society that it attaches us; it is to ourselves.''[16]

In other words, what we often adjudge "good liturgy" or
"meaningful liturgy" does not usually take us beyond the stale-
mate represented by dull, impersonal celebrations. We take part
because we choose to do so, and we choose to do so because we
like it, or it makes us feel good about ourselves, or because we
enjoy praying and singing with others. It gives an evanescent
experience of togetherness, a passing *frisson* of religious excitement, but it doesn't impose the constraints of discipline and commitment. It merely satisfies some obscurely felt need for the time
being but will have to be fresh and different and exciting every
time if it is to keep drawing us back.

I have a thesis, and it is this: that, with the liturgical reforms,
we have moved from the private Mass to the shared celebration,
but we have not yet, by and large, recovered the meaning of public worship.

The *private Mass* was the model adopted by the Missal of Pius V.
A priest and server were all that were needed: the congregation
was dispensable. Even when the congregation was present, it
made little or no difference to the rite; the faithful, for their part,
remained private individuals at prayer. Whether they listened to
the choir, followed the Mass in their missals, or said the Rosary,
their religious privacy and anonymity were never breached.

With Vatican II all this was transformed. Communal celebrations were explicitly preferred over private or quasi-private celebration. The full, active, and conscious participation of the assembled
faithful was required; hence the vernacular, the prayers of the
faithful, congregational singing, lay ministeries, and the rest. All
this was permitted, indeed demanded, but no legislation or instruction could cure us overnight of our ingrained individualism
and privatism. To the degree that liturgical celebrations have been
suffused with individualism, they remain *shared celebrations* rather
than common prayer. To the degree that we are there for our own
private reasons, whether to express our faith or to enjoy singing
and praying together, the liturgy is not yet that of a community,
but merely an assembly of people all "doing their own thing."
However impressive or exhilarating it might be, it remains shared
therapy; it is not yet public domain.

**Private Religion, Individualistic Society, Common Worship**

The Liturgy Constitution, following the definition of the liturgy given by Pius XII, spoke of it as "the full *public worship* . . . performed by the Mystical Body of Jesus Christ, that is, by Head and members."[17] Liturgy is meant to be public worship, then, and its full public character is manifest when the following conditions prevail:

1. It is understood and undertaken as "an action of Christ the priest and of His Body the Church" rather than as something we do on our own terms, "an exercise of the priestly office of Jesus Christ" in which it is our bounden duty, in virtue of our baptismal calling, to participate.

2. Like the redemptive work of Christ which it memorializes and represents, the liturgy is celebrated for the life of the world, not for the personal convenience and consolation of the participants.

3. The sacred duty, *divinum officium*, of celebrating the liturgy is a participation in the unceasing prayer of Christ before God for the salvation of the world and is undertaken with a profound and lively awareness of the larger society which we represent and on whose behalf we offer thanksgiving and intercession to the Father through Christ in the unity of the Holy Spirit.

4. The motivation and direction guiding and shaping the liturgy derives not from our private biographies, but from the larger historical tradition to which we belong and from the eschatological hopes for all humanity which it embodies and projects.

By its nature, then, liturgy is more than shared celebration meeting private needs: it is an act of civic responsibility, of public duty. An anonymous early Christian apologist in his *Epistle to Diognetus* described the relation of the Christian community to the larger society as that of the soul to the body, the source and expression of society's relatedness to God. "Such is the important post to which God has assigned them, and it is not lawful for them to desert it."[18] The local church, then, has public responsibilities, among which not the least important is the offering of public worship.

### III. TOWARDS A PUBLIC WORSHIP

The effects of modernity, and especially of the radical individualism that is its hallmark, have reduced American society to a state of internal incoherence. Such are the conclusions of Robert Bellah and his colleagues, following their study of individualism and

**Mark Searle**

38

commitment in American life.[19] It is not only our natural ecology that is being ravaged by technocracy, they point out, but the human ecology, society itself.

> Human beings have treated one another badly for as long as we have any historical evidence, but modernity has given us a capacity for destructiveness on a scale incomparably greater than in previous centuries. And social ecology is damaged not only by war, genocide, and political repression. It is also damaged by the destruction of the subtle ties that bind human beings to one another, leaving them frightened and alone.[20]

In place of current ideologies of pure undetermined choice—free of tradition, obligation and commitment—we need to recover, Bellah argues, a sense of community, "a 'community of memory' that does not forget its past."

> In order not to forget that past, a community is involved in retelling its story, its constitutive narrative, and in so doing, it offers examples of the men and women who have embodied and exemplified the meanings of the community. . . .
>
> The stories that make up a tradition contain conceptions of character, of what a good person is like, and of the virtues that define such character. But the stories are not all exemplary, not all about successes and achievements. A genuine community of memory will also tell painful stories of shared suffering that sometimes creates deeper identities than success. . . . And if the community is completely honest, it will remember stories not only of suffering received but of suffering inflicted—dangerous memories, for they call the community to alter ancient evils. The communities of memory that tie us to the past also turn us towards the future as communities of hope. They carry a context of meaning that can allow us to connect our aspirations for ourselves and those closest to us with the aspirations of a larger whole and see our own efforts as being, in part, contributions to a common good.[21]

Can our parishes become such "communities of memory" and "communities of hope"? Can our parish liturgies carry a context of meaning that would connect us with the aspirations of the rest of humanity instead of cutting us off from them?

Translated into traditional Catholic vocabulary, such questions become questions of vocation. Can we recover a sense of baptismal vocation, personal and collective, to live as prophets, priests, and servants in the society where we have been placed? In our

**Private Religion, Individualistic Society, Common Worship**

theological tradition, there have always been two dimensions to vocation: the personal and the ecclesial, the inner journey and the public call, neither being complete without the other. This is because, in our tradition, personal vocation is never a purely personal and private matter but finds its definition and scope—whether it be a vocation to a specific kind of ministry or to a particular form of life—within the context of the mission and vocation of the whole Church, which is to serve the kingdom of God in the world. Even a vocation as seemingly personal as a vocation to the contemplative life has always been tested and guided by the Church and justified in terms of the fullness of the Church's own witness. Ordinations and religious professions serve to ritualize this ecclesial call.

Moreover, a vocation is not given and answered once and for all; it is to be received and taken up anew each day. This, in turn, requires communities—capable of reflecting on the world of which they are a part—to discern their vocation in the light of our tradition. In our lifetime, we have witnessed the whole Church engaged in this process at the Second Vatican Council and have seen national synods, pastoral councils, and general congregations of religious orders continuing the process for their own constituencies. At diocean and parish levels such thorough-going efforts to discern our common vocation to be the Church in a specific social context have been less common, but the *communidades de base* in Central and Latin America have offered an influential model. At their best, these and other forms of so-called "intentional community" consist of relatively small groupings of people mutually committed to one another, sharing a critical awareness of and commitment to the cultural, political and economic systems of their society, in continuous and lively contact with other similar communities, and faithfully attentive to the Christian character of their common life.[22]

The recovery of truly public worship is not something that can be achieved by liturgy-planning committees alone. It requires of us all a conversion of outlook and of language, a re-conceiving of the role of the parish and of the Christian community, and a reformulation by each of us of our Christian identity in terms of public vocation rather than private choice.

Karl Rahner describes such a re-formulated identity precisely in reference to liturgy in a little essay entitled "Secular Life and the

**Mark Searle**

Sacraments." After describing how God's grace permeates the whole of human existence and how it was most visibly manifested in Jesus, "in a life made up of everyday things—birth and toil, bravery and hope, failure and death," Rahner argues that the liturgy of the Church is simply the place where we become most profoundly aware of and committed to this "liturgy of the world":

> The world and its history is the terrible and sublime liturgy, breathing death and sacrifice, that God celebrates for himself and allows to be held throughout the free history of men, a history which he himself sustains through the sovereign disposition of his grace. Throughout the whole length and breadth of this collossal history of birth and death, a history on the one hand full of superficiality, folly, inadequacy and hate—and all these "crucify"—a history on the other hand, composed of silent submission, responsibility unto death, mortality and joy, heights and sudden falls: throughout all this there takes place the *liturgy of the world.*

The liturgy of Christ's life and death is the culmination of that liturgy, and it is that liturgy and its redemptive culmination that we celebrate in the liturgy of the Church. The Church is a community of memory, then, because it is called to remember and celebrate not only the memory of Christ but the whole "collossal history of birth and death" which Christ assumed and redeemed when he became one of us.

Such an awareness would profoundly alter the frame of mind with which we enterd into a liturgical celebration. Rahner, in his vivid and inimitable way, describes how such a person might go to Mass:

> He is profoundly aware of the drama into which his life is unceasingly drawn, the drama of the world, the divine Tragedy and the divine Comedy. He thinks of the dying, those facing their end glassy eyed and with the death rattle in their throat, and he knows that this fate has taken up lodging in his own being. He feels in himself the groaning of the creature and the world, their demand for a more hopeful future. He grasps something of the burden born by statesmen, their responsibility for decisions demanding all their courage and yet whose effects will be extending into an unknown future. He bears within himself something of the laughter of children in their unshadowed, future-laden joy: within him resounds also the weeping of the starving children, the agony of the sick, the

**Private Religion, Individualistic Society, Common Worship**

bitterness caused by betrayed love. The dispassionate seriousness of the scientist in his laboratory, the hard determination of those struggling to liberate mankind—all these find their echo in him.[23]

Rahner has much more to say along these lines, and it all deserves our careful and prayerful consideration. While it would certainly be true that someone taking part in the liturgy with such an attitude would be celebrating a public liturgy, it is equally true that such an attitude is not likely to become a hallmark of Catholic worship until our celebrations themselves begin to move beyond the level of "shared celebrations" at which they are currently stuck. To overcome the cultural momentum towards religious individualism, we would need forms of worship which actually cultivated such awareness of the "liturgy of the world." What such forms of worship might look like is not easy to predict, but my own hunch would be that, since the basic elements of our tradition derive from an era in which liturgy was acknowledged as public worship, these new forms would, paradoxically, be rather more traditional than we are currently used to. Perhaps it would be more a matter of style than of form. If so, what would a more public style of worship look like?

Liturgies celebrated as public worship will not be celebrated for the sake of togetherness nor for private intentions. They would be characterized by a certain fixity and solemnity, an objectivity which would constitute an invitation to us to enter in and be shaped by the ritual process. Congregations will not be whisked in and out in forty-five minutes, and missalettes will probably be less in evidence. The proclamation of the scriptural Word would be taken more seriously than it presently is, being heard as a Word addressed more to the community for the sake of the world than to the individuals for their private consolation. In the homily, monologue will yield to dialogue as the Word of God establishes an agenda for the examination of social issues not only during but before and after the liturgy itself. Inspired by the Word, the congregation will become once again a "community of memory," remembering especially the things that our culture forgets: the radical equality of all human beings before God and the centrality in the Chrisian economy of those—like women and children, the unemployed, the handicapped, the sick, the dying, and the unsuccessful—whom society relegates to its margins.

**Mark Searle**

Because it is a "community of memory," the local church will call to mind not only the sins of the world and the failings of individuals but its own collective collusion in those sins so that the celebration of penance will be a genuinely communitarian exercise in prayer, fasting, and examination of community conscience. Marriage will be celebrated not as a personal troth between a man and woman alone but as an ecclesial vocation sanctioned and blessed by the community to bear witness to God's faithful love in the Church and in society. Liturgical ministries will be more closely associated than they now are with community service: ministers of the Word with study and teaching of our tradition and with prophetic analysis of contemporary situations; Eucharistic ministry with care of the sick and with provision for the hungry at home and abroad; the ministry of hospitality with caring for the homeless, visiting the imprisoned, and welcoming the alien and the stranger.

Daily prayer will assume renewed importance in the lives of individuals and communities as an exercise of the priesthood of Jesus Christ on behalf of the world. As in Judaism and early Christianity, fixed forms and times of prayer will be widely known and observed, tying the rhythms of society's day into the economy of our salvation. Psalmody and hymnody will continue to exist side by side, but the hymnody will be marked by the objectivity of the mysteries it celebrates. Its musical forms will be less sentimental and less closely derived from current popular music than is now the fashion. The Church will once again evolve her own musical idiom, reflecting the distinctness of her own identity in the world.

There will be a more profound awareness than we now have of the historic symbols of our community, especially of the symbol of the Body which is the community in Christ. The bread and the cup will weigh heavily as symbols of common destiny, embracing not only the community of the baptised but all who labor for bread and whose sufferings and joys make them participants in the "liturgy of the world." Precisely that awareness that we, as Church, are for the world will make boundaries once again important, defining the community over against a culture it must repudiate. But the boundaries are likely to be drawn somewhat differently from the way in which they are now drawn to include all those who live by their baptism. Water and oil, exorcism and

**Private Religion, Individualistic Society, Common Worship**

blessing will mark those boundaries more sharply, not because we are withdrawing from the world but because, as a community, we are more clear sighted about who we are. Conversely, within the community, awareness of and concern for the larger society will result in common prayer that is not afraid to be specific and does not hide its lack of commitment behind pious generalities. Above all, the weekly celebration of the Eucharist will serve as a weekly renewal of the community's baptismal covenant for the service of God's kingdom in the world, while the observance of the Lord's day will be itself a celebration of our freedom from the impersonal and depersonalizing forces that dominate our post-industrial culture. It will be a day for meeting and remembering, for celebrating and hope: in short, a day for community.[24]

Does this seem so far fetched? Recent pastorals from the American Roman Catholic bishops suggest, both in the topics chosen and in the consultative methodologies employed, that the Church is in process of becoming a public Church once again. Morever, because language and reality never exactly coincide, we are often less individualistic than our ways of talking suggest. The Notre Dame Study of Catholic Parish Life which focused on the kind of average American Catholic parishioners most of us work with found that American Catholics drop easily into the individualistic language of our culture yet still retain considerable community commitment.

The study found, for example, that the single most important reason given by parishioners for their attachment to their parish was not the quality of liturgy or preaching, their family ties, or their love of the church building, but the opportunities their parish offered for community service. Furthermore, it found that the parishioners who claimed the strongest sense of attachment to their parish were those who took advantage of these opportunities to serve and who most regularly interacted with other parish members. As Report #10 notes, ''Opportunities for participation and service, coupled especially with caring pastors and parishioners, are the hallmarks of parish attraction and parishioner attachment.''[25]

Moreover, the study found that, contrary to what one might expect, the sense of community in the thirty-six parishes surveyed was not necessarily stronger in smaller parishes. Three of the five parishes with the strongest sense of community were large, nonethnic, city and suburban parishes. This finding is probably connected with what was discovered about people's sense of attachment—the presence of opportunities for service. "Parishes . . . are not straight-jacketed by the social characteristics of their members. Parishes that recognize the great variations among their members but who find ways to develop interdependence among them, will be rewarded by a greater sense of community than parishes who serve very homogeneous populations."[26]

Where such a sense of commitment and service prevails, public communities of memory and hope are possible. If these committed energies can be harnessed to the service of the wider society instead of merely being turned back into the maintenance of the parish itself, we have the possibility of there emerging what Martin Marty calls "the public Church," a Church which is in the world but is critically reflective about the problems of our society and culture and is committed to working in the public forum for the common good. The emergence of such a public Church is the precondition for public worship and our only antidote to the debilitating effects of privatism, individualism, and massification.

Whether or not that will transform the face of religion in America and so contribute to the transformation of America itself is not for us to know. As Martin Marty says, "It is not for Christians to weigh the odds, but only to be faithful."

## NOTES

1. See David Martin, *A General Theory of Secularization* (New York: Harper and Row, 1978) 31.

2. Bryan Wilson, *Religion in Secular Society* (London: Watts, 1966) 91.

3. Martin, *op. cit.*, 28.

4. Martin Marty, *The Public Church* (New York: Crossroad, 1981) 25.

5. Paulo Freire, *Education for Critical Consciousness* (New York: Continuum, 1973) 34. See also Freire, *Cultural Action for Freedom* (Harmonsworth: Penguin, 1972) 79–82.

6. *Op. cit.*, 87.

7. Thomas Luckmann. *The Invisible Religion. The Problem of Religion in Modern Society* (New York: Macmillan, 1967) esp. 50–68.

8. Robert Bellah *et al.*, *Habits of the Heart. Individualism and Commitment in American Life* (Berkeley: University of California Press, 1984) 142.

**Private Religion, Individualistic Society, Common Worship**

9. *Ibid.* 6.

10. Here following *Habits of the Heart, passim.*

11. Philip Rieff, *The Triumph of the Therapeutic. The Uses of Faith after Freud* (Chicago: University of Chicago Press, 1987) 71.

12. *Op cit.,* 72ff.

13. Robert Bellah, "Civil Religion in America," in Wm. G. McLaughlin and Robert Bellah (eds.), *Religion in America* (Boston: Beacon Press, 1968) 3–23.

14. Martin Marty, *The New Shape of American Religion* (New York: Harper, 1959) 37.

15. *Op. cit.,* 89.

16. Robert Bocock, *Ritual in Industrial Society* (London: George Allen and Unwin, 1974), 56, citing Emil Durkheim, *The Division of Labour in Society.*

17. *Liturgy Constitution,* 7. See Pius XII, *Mediator Dei* (New York: Paulist, 1948) par. 29.

18. *Epistle to Diognetus.* Transl. H. G. Meecham (Manchester: Manchester University Press, 1949) 80.

19. *Habits of the Heart,* 275–96.

20. *Ibid.* 284.

21. *Ibid.* 153.

22. Bernard Lee and Michael Cowan. *Dangerous Memories. House Churches and Our American Story* (New York: Sheed and Ward, 1986) 91–93.

23. Karl Rahner, "Secular Life and the Sacraments," *The Tablet* (6 March 1971) 236–38; (13 March 1971) 267–68.

24. For more specific and imaginative suggestions, see Bernard Lee (general editor), *Alternative Futures for Worship.* 7 vols. (Collegeville: The Liturgical Press, 1987).

25. David C. Leege, *The Parish as Community.* Notre Dame Study of Catholic Parish Life, Report #10 (March 1987) 9.

26. *Ibid.* 5–6.

**Mark Searle**

Peter E. Fink, s.j.

# Liturgy and Spirituality: A Timely Intersection

In December 1973 when the initial meeting of what was to become
the North American Academy of Liturgy was held in Scottsdale,
Arizona, Walter Burghardt set a challenge before us in the form of
a double lament—a challenge to liturgical specialists and to theologians as well. On the one hand, he lamented the loss to theology when it did not take the liturgy of the Church seriously *as a
theological locus*. On the other hand, he lamented the loss to liturgical studies when so few liturgists were profound theologians.

The issue he raised then was the relationship between liturgy
and theology, a relationship which ought to have been obvious
but which had nonetheless been neglected for centuries. Systematic reflection on the sacraments had long since forgotten that
sacraments *are* the liturgy of the Church. The converse was true as
well. Liturgical studies and liturgical piety both had long since forgotten that sacramental theology was in fact the reflective depth of
their own venture. Somehow, theology and liturgy had managed
to develop without much notice of each other.

I like to tell the story of my time in Atlanta when I was invited
to give a presentation to a parish liturgy committee. One member
of the committee who knew me personally was surprised. "I
didn't know you knew anything about liturgy," she said; "I
thought your field was sacraments." When I arrived at Weston
and expressed a desire to teach some sacramental courses, the
question arose: "Why does he want to teach sacraments; we hired
him to teach liturgy." Even in a school of theology, the amnesia
was quite strong.

In the years since Burghardt's address, some advance has been
made in weaving liturgy and theology together or, better, in
realizing that there is a theological depth to the liturgy and a liturgical face to theology. Liturgical folks, at least, have begun to
weave the systematics of sacramental theology into their reflections on the Church at prayer under the new heading of *liturgical
theology*. Systematic theologians, on the other hand, have not been
as convinced that the deepest truth of their trade—be it ecclesiol-
ogy, Christology, the Trinity, revelation, or eschatology—is to be

found not in the inner logic of their own theological method but in the experience of the Church at prayer. In time, that too may come about; that, however, is a challenge for another time.

The challenge we raise here is not unlike Burghardt's challenge of 1973. Although the terms are different, our challenge is one which can be guided by it. Here, we ask about the relationship between spirituality and liturgy, two ventures that have likewise proceeded without much notice of each other and which have both suffered because of their failure to intersect with each other.

In Burghardt's language, let me lament the loss to spirituality when it does not take into account the public prayer of the Church and the loss to liturgy when so few liturgists are themselves profoundly aware of the mystery of God. Let us explore the possible truth of each lament and the thesis that there is a spiritual depth to all study and all practice of Christian liturgy and a liturgical face to any spirituality worthy of the name Christian.

### SPIRITUALITY

Let me talk first of *spirituality*. Spirituality is a large term and quite elusive. It is always hard for me to pin down just what the beast means to those who use the term. It is definitely the "in" word. Put *spirituality* in your brochure, and you are bound to attract a crowd. All sorts of people are into "spiritual direction." All sorts of ministry students want to go into "spirituality." Yet I am not quite sure what it is they want to "go into." After being a spiritual director myself for a number of seminary students, I have to confess that I am not quite sure I know what spiritual direction is either, and I find myself somewhat skeptical of those who are convinced that they do.

Let me play the skeptic's role for a moment and explore the issue as I see it with, I hope, at least a healthy sense of skepticism. My concern is that spirituality can too easily be read through the lens of a psychological paradigm and become quasi-therapy rather than true spiritual growth.

*The Meaning of the Term.* At the very least, one can say that Christian spirituality should have something to do with Christian life, with prayer, and with the profound human journey into the mystery of God which is at the same time the mystery of God made human and the mystery of human life transformed into the

Peter E. Fink, s.j.

48

divine. Spiritualities are frequently associated with people whose own life journey and the language they used to describe it became a guide for the journeys of others.

We can speak, for example, of a Pauline spirituality where Paul urges a life "worthy of our calling," speaks boldly of the mystery of God made manifest in Jesus Christ and of the human journey to walk the same path that Christ himself walked before us, even though it take us through death to resurrection. Paul speaks of what he has seen. We can speak of a Johannine spirituality, that mystical view of the God made flesh that has so deeply influenced Byzantine liturgy and prayer. John had eyes that could gaze upon the torture of the cross and see there the glory of God and the final hope of all human life. John also had such a profound view of the union of people with Christ that he crafted some of the most powerful metaphors in Christian literature: the bread of life, the vine and the branches, the water and the blood from Christ's own side. John, too, speaks about what he has seen.

We can also speak of a spirituality rooted in the vision of some of our greatest saints—Theresa, John of the Cross, Francis, Clare, and, if I may plug my own spiritual family roots, Ignatius of Loyola. All of these men and women have engaged the mystery of God, journeyed deeply into the God made flesh, and discovered that God of mystery deep within the contours of their own human life. They have spoken eloquently of that journey, guiding others into the mystery they had seen and touched and tasted. To embrace a spirituality rooted in such heroes and heroines is to be a disciple, a learner from these women and men, and to choose a life journey into the mystery of God guided by them and inspired by the vision that they have set forth.

We can also speak of "vocation" spirituality, though this tends to be more nebulous without the life witness and vision of heroes and heroines that have given it flesh. It is possible, for example, though much more difficult, to weave a life journey for married persons out of the doctrinal stance that marriage bears witness to the union of Christ and his Church. It is possible—and I'm afraid potentially quite dangerous—to weave a life journey for ordained priests out of the doctrinal stance that the priest stands in the place of Christ. It is possible, though I fear it yields very slender guidance, to weave a life journey for laymen and laywomen on the basis that their vocation is to bring the gospel into the secular world. It has been done, though the witness is not as rich as that which carries the names of our great heroines and heroes.

The point to note is this. Whether we speak of a spirituality associated with persons or of one associated with vocation—however rich or slender—the content of the term always has something to do with Christian life, with prayer, and with the profound human journey into the mystery of God which is at the same time the mystery of God made flesh and the mystery of human life transformed into the divine. Anything short of that is short of true Christian spirituality.

*Current Distortions.* Here is where my skepticism enters in. When I listen to some of the current gurus of spirituality, I hear a language very different from that used by Ignatius or Theresa or Paul. I hear much more the language of personal growth and fulfillment, of recognition and affirmation, of "feeling good about one's self," than I do of companionship with God born of contemplation, of life transformed through suffering and injustice freely embraced, of death to oneself in order that others might live.

I weep when the Enneagram or the Myers-Briggs analysis replaces the almost erotic intimacy with Christ described by John of the Cross in his "Dark night of the soul," or the stunning challenge to discipleship and companionship presented in some of the great Ignatian meditations on the mystery of Christ. The psychological tools are fun and even helpful, but they create a fascination with oneself and in the end leave us alone with that fascination. I grow very sad when the paradoxical wisdom of our heroines and heroes is replaced by the strategies and stages of the psychological paradigm. A language that was once very large and awesomely beautiful has been transformed into a language that is very self-centered and very small.

The same thing happens when I engage in spiritual direction myself and ask my directees what it is they are looking for. Essentially they are looking for what the gurus promise: personal growth and fulfillment, recognition and affirmation, a good feeling about one's self. They all know their Myers-Briggs letters, and most know their Enneagram numbers. But very few know the language of companionship with God born of contemplation or transformation of life born of suffering and injustice freely embraced.

Peter E. Fink, S.J.

Very few speak of dying to themselves that others might live. I once remarked to a friend in Cambridge that I was astonished at how much time these ministry students spent watching themselves grow.

May I be allowed one case study as a single example. On the eve of his ordination, after I had heard his confession, I asked a brother Jesuit what spirituality he wanted most to hear from God. He answered, "That God loves me and accepts me." I looked at him and said, "That's easy, but I think God wants to say much more to you. I think God wants to speak of the people you are going to serve, of the compassion God wants you to bring to them, of the vision God wants to awaken in them through you. I think God has greater desires of you and wants you to have larger desires than you do."

The spirituality of Ignatius, as most of you know, involves a journey that has as a *first* phase the freedom of living as a loved sinner. But that is just its first phase. The *second* one is the passion to serve the redemption of the world with Christ who is its redeemer. The *third* phase is the compassion which allows the crucifixion itself to unfold within one's own life. And the *fourth* phase is the true freedom to embrace the world and all that is in it through the eyes and with the affections of the risen Christ. How sadly small it is for a Jesuit, on the eve of his ordination, to seek only to be loved and accepted by God.

I fear that I very much embrace the lament I have adapted from Burghardt that spirituality does indeed suffer loss when it allows the psychological paradigm to be its guide. How different it would be if spirituality would intersect with the public prayer of the Church.

The liturgy of the Church does not allow us the self-doubts that much of the contemporary spirituality seems to make its stock in trade. The liturgy of the Church assumes that we are sinners who belong in the presence of God. "We thank you that you count us worthy to stand before you and serve you" (Eucharistic Prayer II). It does not allow us, unless we ourselves distort the text, to be self-centered, self-conscious, self-concerned. The liturgy of the Church stretches us to be for others—not for ourselves—from the liturgy of initiation where even our own renewal of baptismal promises is not done for ourselves but in context with the baptism of others, right through to the liturgy of Christian burial where

**Liturgy and Spirituality**

the proclamation of resurrection is boldly made that we may, in Paul's words, "comfort one another."

The liturgy of the Church, with all its many moods and rhythms—some which make us feel good, some which do not—takes the human journey where the psychological paradigm cannot take it. It takes us beyond letters and beyond numbers, beyond self-fascination and beyond self-fulfillment into the mystery of God where the God-become-flesh is the center and where human life, yours and mine, is transformed into the divine.

### LITURGY

Let me turn to the second lament, the loss to liturgy when its ministers, practitioners, and theologians do not bring spiritual depth to the task.

*Goal: The Renewal of Christian Life.* The renewal called for by Vatican II was, as we all know, only in a first phase the reform of liturgical texts. That part of the task can be easily dispatched. It has, in large measure, already been accomplished. The deeper renewal envisioned by the Council was a renewal of faith or, in the Council's own words, "an ever increasing vigor to the Christian life of the faithful" (Liturgy Constitution, 1). The aim, as I have come to describe it, was to recapture the richest expressions of our faith lodged in the heritage of the Church universal, East and West, and unleash that richness upon the people of today.

For example, it was deemed urgent to open up the riches of scripture rather than content our prayer with only a meager collection of biblical texts. It was considered important, too, to recapture the language of the Spirit of God's agent in transforming the human heart and in particular the primary Eucharistic Spirit prayer, "that all of us who share in the body and blood of Christ be brought together in unity" (Eucharistic Prayer II). It was considered essential that our symbols speak lavishly, not gingerly; that bodies be immersed in water; that oil be lavishly spread; that food look and act like food. Finally, it was held to be the highest goal that people engage the mystery of God by actively participating in the signs and symbols, the words and the prayers, the songs and the gestures that constitute our liturgical prayer. "In the restoration of the liturgy, the full and active participation of all the people is the aim to be considered above all else" (Liturgy Constitution, 14).

**Peter E. Fink, S.J.**

52

If there is a single sentence in the Constitution on the Sacred Liturgy that has captured my own heart and mind in regard to the spiritual depth of the Church's prayer, it is this: "It is through the liturgy, especially, that the faithful are enabled to express in their lives and manifest to others the mystery of Christ and the real nature of the true Church" (Liturgy Constitution, 2). To bring to expression the reality of Jesus Christ, his stance before the God he names *Abba*, and his stance before the people he names "not servants but friends": this is the true depth of the Church's Prayer. It is the true depth into which the Church's prayer invites all who pray.

Now let me play the skeptic once again. If spirituality, without the corrective of the public prayer of the Church, is in danger of yielding to a psychological paradigm, my experience tells me that liturgy, without the corrective of a true and solid spirituality, can all too easily be taken over by the dynamics of a political paradigm. We have seen it in the past when the liturgy was used by Charlemagne and Pippin before him to unify the Empire or by the post-reformation Roman Church to hold together the remnants of an increasingly fragmented Church. The current reform was supposed to be different. The question is: is it?

*Primacy of Unity.* Let me focus my skepticism in one place only, on what I take to be the most remarkable recoveries in the reformed Eucharistic liturgy of Vatican II—the request for unity among those who partake of the body and blood of Christ. It is quite explicit in all of the new Eucharistic prayers of the Roman Sacramentary and in most of those employed by the other churches of the West in their own liturgical reforms. Judging from the earliest Eucharistic texts we have, that of the *Didache* and the anaphora of Hippolytus, unity was the first desire of the Church to be expressed in Eucharistic prayer. It was only later replaced by desire for personal benefit and still later by prayer for the conversion of bread and wine.

With the restoration comes a truer sense of communion, not so much Jesus coming to *me* as Jesus in our midst setting us in relation to each other. This prayer restores the Eucharist as the primary sacrament of reconciliation, the primary place where Paul's plea to the Corinthians is to be realized: "that there be no dissensions among you" (1 Cor 1:10). Eucharist is the sacrament that heals division, not the one that causes it.

The good news is that the Eucharistic liturgy has become a lot more fun for people. People enjoy coming together in a way that was not in great evidence before Vatican II. The kiss of peace has taken hold, sometimes to orgy proportions. People talk in church before, after, and sometimes even during the Eucharistic celebration. There is a friendliness in evidence that is a refreshing change from the days when "sister" and "father" hovered over us making sure that we behaved. Visitors and strangers are introduced and welcomed. A new ministry of hospitality has arisen in many places. And Roman Catholic priests are joining their Reformation colleagues in standing outside the church after the liturgy to greet the people and be greeted by them. "Loved your sermon, Father."

But there is bad news as well. In many places, so my own experience tells me, liturgy has become a divisive force, not a unitive force. There are many hands seeking to control its ways rather than to liberate us to enter its ways fully and freely. I fear that liturgy has become once again a political tool, making points and negotiating issues, rather than a profound journey into the mystery of Christ or a transformation of the human heart into the ways of God.

Witness bishops insisting that the people kneel during the Eucharistic prayer, even during the Easter time when classically kneeling is forbidden, in order to preserve the distinction between the ordained and unordained. They don't seem to have realized that you cannot pray *doxology* or sing a great *Amen* on your knees. It doesn't work. The body won't let it work.

Witness that the insistence on a variety of ministers working together has yielded new battles over turf. God help the presider who steals a one-liner from the deacon, the lay reader who presumes to read the gospel, or, most tragic of all, the woman who presumes to have her feet washed on Holy Thursday, in some dioceses at least.

Witness the fate, in some places at least, of the genuine and good concern that the liturgy use inclusive, not exclusive, language. It becomes almost an obsession with men and women both guarding the language so strenuously that all hell breaks loose should a presider or reader or anyone else simply slip up.

Peter E. Fink, S.J.

*Control: A Subversion of Unity.* Now all of the above difficulties began with a good idea. It is important for our prayer that the presider in some way stand out and not simply be "one of the crowd." It is important that the many ministries be on display. It is important that the language we use draw both women and men into the prayer of the Church and not leave anyone deliberately alienated from that prayer. Yet when the good idea gets drawn into the political paradigm and hands seek to control the liturgy rather than invite people into its gracious ways, it no longer serves the Church at prayer. It begins to tear us apart instead.

It is at this point that we need to hear the wisdom of our heroines and heroes, and with force. Our heroes and heroines of the spiritual life never imagined themselves in control of the ways of God. They were always vulnerable to God's gracious approach. The liturgy, too—if it will serve God's ways among us—must find us vulnerable to its power. It is not a tool in our hands to serve our own issues and demands, whatever they be. It is, or should be, God's gracious approach to us, a gift to unify us beyond the divisions that are caused by our issues and demands. If I may adapt a phrase of one of my intellectual heroes, Paul Ricoeur, liturgy will heal, but it must humble us first.

I must take exception to a remark by my esteemed colleague Aidan Kavanagh, who once asserted that liturgy was rite, not prayer. It is my deepest conviction that, if liturgy *is not* prayer, it is not worth doing, and it may well be a dangerous weapon in the hands of those who control it. If liturgy is not prayer, there is no point in our being here, no point in trying to imagine how spirituality and liturgy may intersect. If liturgy is not prayer, they don't.

But, if it *is* prayer, if there is a valid intersection between spirituality and liturgy, the price we will be asked to pay for successful liturgy is high. It will be nothing less than the journey which the liturgy itself enacts, the journey into the mystery of God made flesh, the transformation of human life into the divine, and the death of oneself and all one's issues and concerns in order that others may live. Liturgy will heal us, but it must humble us first.

In the first part, I shared the lament I adapted from Burghardt: *spirituality does indeed suffer loss when it allows the psychological paradigm to be its guide and not the public prayer of the Church.* In this part, I share the other lament as well: *liturgy does indeed suffer loss*

**Liturgy and Spirituality**

*when it allows a political paradigm to be its guide and not the spiritual journey which our great mystics have taken before us.*

### A LITURGICAL SIDE TO CHRISTIAN SPIRITUALITY

Let us go now to the intersection of liturgy and spirituality and ask first of all how liturgy might protect spirituality from yielding itself to the psychological paradigm. There are many points I'd like to explore, but I will content myself with just two theses.

The first is that *the language of all authentic Christian spiritualities is* public language *and cannot be privatized without doing it violence.* Public language belongs to a community of people. It maps the public vision of that community and shapes both its public life and the prayer of its members. It is large language, large enough to allow a diversity of people to hold their lives together in a common vision and for a common task. The language of Christian spiritualities is, in fact, itself liturgical or at least quasi-liturgical in both the way it behaves and the purpose it serves. Because of this, the liturgy of the Church, which is *the* public language of the Church and which likewise cannot be privatized without violence to itself, can serve as a model for all more specific spiritualities within the Church.

My second thesis is less a question of modelling and more one of direct interaction. I propose that *every spirituality can and should intersect with the liturgy of the Church,* each on its own terms, and if it cannot, there is something unauthentic—and perhaps dangerous—about the spirituality in question.

*Spirituality as Public Language.* Let me explore the first thesis, spirituality as public language, from personal history with a focus on the Spiritual Exercises of St. Ignatius. These Exercises which belong to the Church and not just to the Jesuits contain the life-blood of Jesuit or Ignatian spirituality.

When I entered the Society of Jesus in 1956, the accepted means of employing these Exercises was the preached retreat. A few of these retreats were brilliant. Many more went from mediocre to "okay." Some were disasters. But all employed the same common structure, the same common patterns, the same common language. Even when all they did was give us something to joke about later on, we had a common language in which to appreciate the humor.

**Peter E. Fink,** S.J.

56

As public language, the Exercises shaped our vision, inspired our dreams, motivated our choices; the vision they set forth allowed us to see a great diversity of lifestyles and apostolates born of the same source and reflecting the same passion for the "greater glory of God." The teacher, the politician, the scientist, the theologian, and the giver of retreats all had in their grasp the language to hold their ideals together: service of the kingdom, in the footsteps of the crucified savior, toward the transformation of human life and human history seen through the eyes of the risen Christ.

About halfway through my life as a Jesuit, a different medium to employ these Exercises was recaptured: the directed retreat. It was hailed as good news, and rightly so. The directed retreat provided for individual guidance through these Exercises and unleashed the power of Spirit discernment, which is the stuff of individual choice and decision, in a way and to an extent undreamed of in the preached retreat. The shift from preached retreat to directed retreat was rapid and total.

The shift, however, had a dark side to it which some of us are only now beginning to notice. As the once-public medium of the Exercises went private, the once-public language went private as well. We lost the Exercises as a language of common discourse. They no longer served to shape our common vision or to forge our common dreams. Without the corrective of public discourse, even the great meditations of the Exercises became functions of personal growth and no longer the language to shape dreams and visions.

I began to notice this when what I call "weasel words" from our congregation documents began to serve for our younger Jesuits what the Exercises once served for us. Service of faith and justice became the "in" phrase, and unless we were serving faith and justice as those who most adopted the phrase proposed, there was something suspect about our life as a Jesuit. A shrinkage was taking place.

I am not against service of faith and justice. The phrase just pales so pitifully next to "service of the kingdom under the banner of Christ." Service of faith and justice is a "cause," service of Christ and his kingdom is a "mission." The service of faith and justice turns my gaze to the poor and oppressed and to those without faith, but all it gives me with which to respond is my

**Liturgy and Spirituality**

own meager compassion and my own very small project. That is a more subtle form of self-centeredness. Service of Christ and his kingdom turns my gaze to the poor and oppressed and those without faith as well, and to many, many more. But it gives me more than my own compassion; it gives me *companionship,* and it gives me the vision of Christ and the passion of Christ to challenge and shape my own. Service of faith and justice may or may not lead me to the worship of God. Service of Christ and his kingdom is the worship of God.

The practical end may, and possibly should be, the same. The path to that end, however, is quite different. The language of congregation documents is simply no substitute for the large language of spiritual vision.

There is, as I say, something liturgical about the public langauge of any spirituality. It is public. It shapes and becomes the work of the people. It belongs to the community and cannot be usurped or distorted by any individual without the community rightly raising critical voices. Its vision is large, large enough to encompass many styles of living it out. And because it engages people not merely in an apostolic task but even more in the mission and journey of Jesus Christ, it involves these same people in the worship of God and the sanctification of human life and human history. The challenge of the Church's liturgy to any spirituality is to keep its language public, to keep its vision large, and to remind it that its full and final task is the worship of God and the transformation of humanity. Liturgy will keep spirituality from becoming self-centered and small.

*Interaction of Spirituality and Liturgy.* I can explore the second point, the interaction of spirituality and liturgy, more briefly, this time using personal observation as well as personal history. Forgive me if I stay with the Spiritual Exercises of Ignatius which is the world I know best.

From time to time, directors of retreats find the liturgy of the Church embarrassing, awkward, even intrusive. A director is taking someone through meditations on her or his own sinfulness, and along comes a resurrection reading or a joyful feast. Or a director is guiding a retreatant through a meditation on generous service, and the scriptures for the day are full of gloom and foreboding. The director decides to suppress a feast or change a reading to fit the retreatant.

Peter E. Fink, S.J.

I have long felt that such tampering with the liturgy during a retreat shows great ignorance of both the retreat dynamic and the liturgy. There is something wrong when the Church's prayer is seen to interfere with the prayer of one of its members. It also betrays a false understanding of his role on the part of the director, as though the director had to control the environment of prayer for those who were engaging the mystery of God in their own lives.

During my own tertianship retreat when I was struggling through the second week and a woman religious was entering the third week, along came a liturgical feast with a fourth-week resurrection reading. It was as though the Church did not even care that we were making the Spiritual Exercises of Ignatius. But really it didn't matter. For me, and I hope for her, God found two different voices by which to speak in our hearts, and it was after all God, and not the "topic of the retreat," who was important.

The liturgy of the Church, left alone, may clash with the designs of the director; it cannot clash with the designs of God. And it reminds the director, or any other weaver of the language of a specific spirituality, that all such exercises and all such language are at the service of a mystery which no one can control. Direct interaction of the liturgy of the Church with any spirituality keeps that spirituality honest and free to be a language which directs us into the mystery of God.

A SPIRITUAL SIDE TO CHRISTIAN LITURGY

What of the other question: a spiritual side to the liturgy? If liturgy can help save spirituality from the psychological paradigm by keeping its language public and its dynamic not only one of human growth but of growth into the mystery of God, how shall spirituality in turn save liturgy from its own temptation to yield itself to the political paradigm?

I propose that the liturgy itself can reveal the answer if we allow it to reveal to us the proper approach we must take to it. Liturgy will reveal itself to be prayer and show us the kind of prayer it is, if we listen carefully. Vatican II says that the liturgy expresses the mystery of Christ, that in the liturgy *we* express the mystery of Christ, and we cannot express that mystery in our own flesh and blood without being drawn into its dynamic and its depth.

**Liturgy and Spirituality**

All liturgy begins with the liturgy of the Word, the proclamation of God's agenda, God speaking God's own agenda in the person of Jesus Christ. All liturgy begins in the presence of God who sets forth *the* Word made flesh. And Word calls forth response.

Just to hear the Word requires a humility that sets aside all other agenda that might stand in its way. Liturgy heals, but it must humble us first. It demands that we put on what we hear, make it our own, give it our own flesh and blood. All that follows the Word proclamation is response: our response, God's response, our surrender to what God's response makes of us. Proper response to the Word takes us into the agenda of God where God, not we ourselves, determines the outcome. The classic Eucharistic pieces of offertory, consecration, and communion, which have their counterparts in each of our sacraments, are neither more nor less than this: our response, God's response, our surrender to what God's response makes of us.

Whatever issue, concern, or agenda we bring, which in the political paradigm is the task to be accomplished, needs to be set into the Word proclaimed in order to find there its proper definition. Our task is not to accomplish but to surrender to the accomplishment of God, which is never a *fait accompli* which we passively accept but an on-going action which we are invited to co-act with God. Our task is to allow our own small agenda to be enlarged, redefined, and transformed into God's agenda which we will in freedom take to be our own.

We are all familiar with the newly rediscovered definition of liturgy as the work of the people. It is certainly an advance over an understanding of liturgy that sees it only as the work of a few. But that definition of liturgy—as the work of the people—has a fatal flaw, and it is that flaw which renders it vulnerable to the political paradigm. It tends to put *us,* and not the mystery of God, in control.

If we listen to the liturgy itself, it does not name itself as the work of the people but as the work of God in the midst of and within the people. God names the agenda. God draws us into God's agenda; God transforms us for the task of God's agenda and redefines that task in a way, and to an extent, that we ourselves could not dream or imagine. If we listen to the liturgy itself, it will show itself to be about that same journey of human transformation of which the mystics speak so eloquently.

**Peter E. Fink,** S.J.

If the challenge of liturgy at the intersection of liturgy and spirituality is to keep the language of spirituality public and honest, the challenge of spirituality at that same intersection is to keep liturgy humble and true. We are humbled when we realize that—our newly rediscovered definition of liturgy notwithstanding—liturgy is not the work of the people; it is first and foremost the *work of God in the people* transforming them, us, and all human life into God's own glory. Those of us engaged in the liturgy of the Church as practitioners, ministers, or theologians need the wisdom and insight of true spirituality to illuminate that transformation and instruct us in its ways.

### CONCLUSION

A keynote address should not really have a conclusion. The proper conclusion is the workshop it keynotes. But it must, at least, come to an end. I entitled this address, ''Liturgy and Spirituality: a Timely Intersection,'' and it is this intersection which will occupy us in the days ahead. Let me end with two propositions that may well serve as a summary of what I have tried to say. The first is this: the vision set forth in the Church's liturgy is the primary vision that must shape any authentic Christian spirituality and the primary context in which any specific spirituality must understand itself. Liturgy provides a paradigm for all spirituality. And the second proposition is this: the Church's liturgy sets forth a vision which is itself a spirituality, a journey into the mystery of God made human and the mystery of men and women transformed into the divine. Liturgy needs the eyes of women and men who have known in their own lives this profound transforming journey of prayer if liturgy is to see itself and that journey correctly.

Don E. Saliers

# Liturgy Teaching Us To Pray:
# Christian Liturgy and Grateful Lives of Prayer

*Rejoice always, pray constantly,*
*give thanks in all circumstances;*
*for this is the will of God in*
*Christ Jesus for you.* (1 Thess 5:16-18)

Christian prayer, whether in the gathered assembly or in solitude, is first and last praising and giving thanks to God. It is much more, of course, but these modes are primary. The living practice of prayer, of people praying together and alone, shapes and expresses the distinctive character of gratitude and thanksgiving in Christian faith and life together. Our focus is on the continuing dialogue of prayer which shapes and expresses human community in the particular affections, attitudes, and ways of intending the world which the liturgy, in all its range, signifies and evokes.

All of us have learned to speak of Christian liturgy as the assembly gathered about the book, the font, and the table of the Lord to corporately enact—in word and sign-act, in symbol and song—the Gospel: to participate in the mystery of God's self-giving. We have come in these past two decades to teach catechumens and to speak to one another of a liturgical life which involves social relatedness and our "full, conscious, active" participation in that liturgical life. All this has confronted us with new questions and has plunged us into the depths of symbol and ritual action, reacquainting us with forgotten or neglected primary experiences of our need for transcendence and for emotional range in common prayer and life.

At the same time, much preoccupation with "spirituality" in recent years has focused, at the popular level, on self-awareness and on enriching our interior and personal lives through prayer, discipline, and meditation. So our question is not simply "How can liturgy teach us to pray?" but rather "How can liturgy teach us to pray in a culture of narcissism which shapes religious sensibility?" What are the relations between liturgy as prayer and our *becoming prayerful* when much spiritual renewal is but warmed-over and

**Don E. Saliers**

62

privatized Pietism or merely the sentimental rehearsal of middle-class values and aspirations? I am inadequate to provide answers. I confess complicity in the culture which provides modes of communication—musical and otherwise—employed in liturgical celebration. I can only trace some primary themes at the intersection of liturgical prayer and becoming prayerful. Perhaps this is but a gloss on Johannes Metz's contemporary reminder: "Those who pray are not alone; they form part of a great historical company: prayer is a matter of historical solidarity."[1]

Prayer is the on-going living relationship of mutuality and awareness between humanity and God. We cannot neglect the human dimensions of praying. Metz's paraphrase of Ernst Bloch's comment speaks to this: "Prayer is at times like the daydream of that home whose light shines in our childhood, yet a home where none of us has ever been."[2] What prompts such a yearning? How are we convinced this home exists? Consider an instance or two. When we gather with friends eating, drinking and talking into the evening, little by little stories unfold and images of life emerge—of loss and gain, hurt and healing, promises made and broken, of years quickly sped and life not turning out as we had expected. Toward the end of the evening someone remarks, "Wouldn't it be wonderful to be in a place where you could share everything and be able to live with others knowing they know, because you were at home—No more a stranger or a guest, but like a child at home?" Or the news from the hospital is not good. Relatives begin to gather—a sister from Chicago, a brother from St. Louis, an aunt and uncle from Florida. One child has been keeping lonely vigil at the mother's bedside and now everyone is gathering, crowded together in the room when she takes her last breath. They form a circle out of some primordial impulse. "Gather her home," you say quietly. . . .

Christian liturgy may be defined as the on-going prayer, proclamation, and life of Jesus Christ—a sacrifice of thanksgiving and praise—offered to God in and through his Body in the world. That is, Christian liturgy is our response to the self-giving of God in, with, and through the One who leads us in prayer. The community is called into being to continue that prayer on behalf of the whole world. So we must continue to gather in praise and thanksgiving about the book, the baptismal font, and the Eucharistic table in order to know a home. This extended definition highlights the Christological nature of Christian worship and its dynamic historical and temporal character. Yet it opens the way for a discussion of the relation between gratitude and God's grace. As Geoffrey Wainwright has trenchantly observed:

> In worship we receive the self-giving love of God, and the test of our thankfulness is whether we reproduce that pattern of self-giving in our daily relationships with other people. Of course, the test already begins with our attitudes and behaviour as brothers and sisters in the liturgical assembly. . . .[3]

We shall return to this linkage between liturgy and ethics later.

SOME PRELIMINARIES

Before analyzing how specific liturgical prayers teach us to pray, we must make two points. *First, Christian prayer and prayerfulness can be distinguished from the reciting of texts of prayers.* As David Steindl-Rast reminds us, "Sooner or later we discover that prayers are not always prayer."[4] His point is that prayer is on-going communion with God, whereas prayers are texts we pray, whether in the written or oral tradition. What makes our prayers *prayer* is whole-hearted attentiveness or attunement to God in and through the utterances. The intention and the state of mind of prayer, Steindl-Rast terms "recollection," drawing upon classical Catholic tradition. We may analyze prayer texts and interpret liturgical actions yet miss the heart of the matter. Prayer in the Christian tradition is not indifferent, passionless, or distracted. The thanksgiving offered in response to God, as Romano Guardini observed, "consists in accepting life, with ever-growing awareness, as God's gift."[5]

Prayer as living communion with God, as awareness of existence as divine gift is beyond the language of liturgical prayer texts; it is the very pattern of affection and intention in the lives of those who pray. I do not desire to construct a dualism of inner experience and outward language and ritual act, but to show how we learn the affections of gratitude and praise by means of such language as ritual gesture. We learn *how* to give thanks and praise to God by coming to participate in the reality referred to in the descriptions and ascriptions of God as creator, judge, redeemer, sustainer, and consummate lover of all creation. This requires conceptual determinacy, not mere feeling or inchoate experience.

**Don E. Saliers**

64

Praying in the Christian context moves through understanding the memories of the Church witnessed to in Scripture, the narratives, images, and depictions of the divine life in concrete human terms. This is why, among other things, love of God requires love of neighbor. It is also why there is a constant anthropomorphic tension in language used to speak of God: "Father of mercies," "shepherd," "searcher of hearts." Such learning about God from participation in liturgical action can never be a matter of didactic content either; coming to know God is personal encounter, not cognitive mastery of texts.

*The second point concerns the manner in which human beings acquire a capacity for sustained gratitude.* This gratitude to the Divine for the gift of life and the benefits of the divine self-giving in history is not a mysterious "inner experience" so much as it is a pervasive attunement to the world in all its beauty, terror, and mystery. In this sense, human maturity is involved. A deepening capacity for gratitude and thankfulness leads to a more comprehensive sense of truth about how things are. At the same time, thankfulness to God requires a re-configuration of our natural desires. We may say that Christian prayer, so far as it is speaking God's name in praise and thanksgiving, is part of the discovery of our own humanity. The classical definition of worship as the glorification of God and the sanctification of all that is human suggests this. There are anthropological consequences. Let us speak of prayer, then, as a double journey—both toward the mystery of God who invites relationship and also into the deep places of our own human self-understanding. This leads Guardini to say:

> It is therefore of the utmost importance that we should learn to give thanks. We must do away with the indifference which takes all things for granted, for nothing is to be taken for granted— everything is a gift. Not until man [sic] has understood this will he truly be free.[6]

We find in the texts of Christian prayers of thanksgiving the opposite of indifference; they are also an invitation to human maturity. Learning to attend to God and to intend all things to God gives us the freedom for spontaneity in relation to the world, for being "surprised by joy." Understanding ourselves and the whole human family as recipients of the gifts of God's good creation, sustaining mercy and justice, is to re-orient ourselves to the world

**Teaching Us To Pray**

and to other human beings with a continuous gratitude which renders both the praying and the living as response to grace. The central mystery of gratitude in the Christian context is the re-ordering of relations between creature and the Creator. We find this most intensely in the texts of Eucharistic prayers. While the pattern recalls God's being and his specific acts in history, the focus is upon God's self-giving in Jesus Christ who is taken to be the recapitulation and the paradigmatic manifestation of the divine self-giving. In the Prayer of General Thanksgiving from the *Book of Common Prayer*, God is thanked for "our creation, preservation, and for all the blessings of this life," but chiefly for the "redemption of the world in Jesus Christ." The deep affections which are formed in continuing to pray this prayer are at one and the same time interior—relating to desire and a range of other affections such as compassion, repentance, and joy—and relational—to the social and historical contexts in which human beings live. Authentic prayer forms us in an affectional understanding of the truth about how things are.

EUCHARISTIC PRAYERS:
MODEL OF PRAISE AND THANKSGIVING

In what follows we will see how the Eucharistic prayers are the most intensive and extensive form of praise and thanksgiving in the Christian tradition. A full analysis is, of course, not possible here. Suffice it to say that the Eucharistic prayers which emerged very early in the Christian tradition contain all the modes of prayer within the framework of thanksgiving: praise, adoration, confession, invocation, supplication, and eschatological doxology. We turn first to two of the most significant early forms of the Eucharistic prayer as a way of illuminating the themes and proposals advanced thus far.

The earliest Christians prayed to God and gave thanks with the language and gestures inherited from Judaism. The synagogue and domestic-meal liturgies and, to a lesser extent, the Temple rites provided fundamental images and basic patterns by which the earliest Christian communities addressed praise and thanks to God. The writings of the New Testament reflect this. These writings were themselves generated by the prayer and worship in the daily lives of the churches in the first two centuries.[7] In the Acts of the Apostles, the author tells us:

**Don E. Saliers**

And they devoted themselves to the apostles' teaching and fellowship, to the breaking of bread and the prayers. . . . And day by day, attending the temple together and breaking bread in their homes, they partook of food with glad and generous hearts, praising God and having favor with all the people.[8]

This is a picture of the earliest Christian community in Jerusalem. There is an obviously close connection between the structure and rhythm of prayer and the fellowship and ritual action, especially in the continuation of praise and thanksgiving at daily meals as well as in the Temple. Some scholars have seen in the phrase, "the breaking of bread and prayers," a reference to an embryonic Eucharistic rite. While by no means Eucharistic in the full ritual sense of the term, these passages nevertheless give evidence of inherited patterns of thanksgiving now linked with the teachings of the apostles about Jesus' life, death, and resurrection. This is clear from the literary context in Acts where this description follows Peter's extended sermon in the second chapter concerning the meaning of Jesus' life in light of the crucifixion and resurrection.

The points of continuity with Judaism are strikingly evident in prayer texts from the document called the *Didache* or "Teachings of the Lord, given to the nations through his Apostles." Written at the close of the first century or the beginning of the second, the *Didache* records the following texts in chapter nine:

1. With regard to the prayer of thanksgiving *(eucharistia)*, offer it in this fashion.
2. First, for the cup: "We thank you, our Father, for the holy vine of David your servant, which you have revealed to us through Jesus your servant. Glory be yours through all ages!
3. Then for the bread broken: "We thank you, our Father, for the life and knowledge you have revealed to us through Jesus your servant. Glory be yours through all ages!
4. Just as the bread broken was first scattered on the hills, then was gathered and became one, so let your Church be gathered from the ends of the earth into your kingdom, for yours is glory and power through Jesus Christ for all ages!"[9]

There are parallel prayers in chapter 10, one of which reads:

All powerful Master, you created all things for your name's sake, and you have given food and drink to the children of men for their enjoyment, so that they may thank you. On us, moreover, you have bestowed a spiritual food and drink that lead to eternal life, through Jesus your servant.[10]

Anyone even slightly familiar with Jewish traditions of prayer recognizes the close connection with the blessing prayers prayed at meals and the language used by the *Didache*. The language and the gestures of blessing and thanking God in the meal *berakoth* (especially the Birkat ha-Mazon) echoes in these prayers. The use of the Greek word *pais* ("servant" or "child") to refer to Jesus is evidence of the antiquity of the prayer forms cited here.[11] The significance of the linkages between the actual prayer formularies of various meal *berakoth* and the emerging pattern of prayers at the Christian Eucharist is far too complex to investigate here. For our purposes it must suffice to observe the intrinsic relation of the inherited Jewish prayers of praise, blessing, and thanksgiving to the Eucharistic prayer and ritual actions. The most striking point about the *Didache* is that it appropriates the pattern of a Jewish household meal in which the blessing of God for wine and bread preceded the meal and a series of prayers concluded the meal. This final prayer was, in fact, a series of four blessings. The *first* blessing praised God as ruler of the universe who gives food to all creatures. In the *Didache*, chapter 10,3, we find the additional note of thanks for the "spiritual food and drink leading to eternal life" through Jesus. The *second* blessing of the concluding meal *berakoth* focused upon the acts of God in leading Israel out from slavery. In the *Didache*, the Christian community also praised and thanked God for mighty acts in history, but the focus is upon the "knowledge, faith and immortality" revealed in Jesus who is described by St. Paul as "our Passover" in his Corinthian correspondence some thirty years earlier.

The *third* benediction prayed for mercy on Jerusalem and the lineage of David. The *Didache* prayer focuses upon the Church, supplicating God to "gather it from the four winds . . . into your kingdom." This is directly parallel to the "gathering of the dispersed children of Israel" in the final table benedictions—an eschatological yearning for full restoration. The *fourth* benediction in the meal prayers consisted of a lengthy series of petitions which constantly addressed God as "good and benevolent" or the "kindly lover" of humanity. In the *Didache* prayers of chapter 10,4, we encounter a short formula which may imply a series of

**Don E. Saliers**

68

spontaneous petitions which are prayed gratefully: "Above all we thank you because you are almighty. Glory be yours through all ages!" The end of the chapter states simply: "Allow the prophets to give thanks as much as they wish."

FUNDAMENTAL INSIGHTS

From this brief excursion into one significant source of the earliest Christian Eucharistic manner of prayer, four points can be drawn which will permeate the remainder of our discussion. *First*, the patterns—the "deep structures"—of Christian liturgical thanksgiving are indelibly Jewish in origin and cannot be understood without knowing their antecedents.[12] *Secondly*, God is praised and most especially thanked by the remembrance of mighty acts as well as specific benevolences in creation, for example, the fruit of the vine and bread from the earth. The connections between creation and history are placed in the context of the glory of God's own being. Hence, praise for what God has done must not merely be an expression of the beneficiaries' "blessings" but also of the sheer acknowledgement of the glory of God in the mystery of God's own self. This is later to develop into a distinction between thanks for God *pro nobis*, "for the creatures," and praise to God *in se* or *a se*, God "in himself." In the *third* place the Christian community from the beginning included the mediating role of Jesus in the very act of praise and thanksgiving. The distinctive fact of *eucharistia* was "in and through Jesus." The *Didache* speaks of "servant" or "child," while the characteristic ending "through Jesus Christ our Lord" developed in the doxologies and benedictions used in the Pauline letters and elsewhere.

A *fourth* point emerges: all petitions and intercessions are part of an eschatological dimension of all praise and thanksgiving. Not only is there a transfer of the eschatological petitions for Jerusalem and the scattered children of Israel to the community whose identity is marked by the person and work of Jesus of Nazareth, but the very act of prayer as petition or intercession for the whole world is an implicit prayer that the kingdom or final rule of God may come to the whole world. Corroborating evidence is found in the initial petition of the Lord's Prayer, echoing its antecedent in the ancient *Kaddish* from the Jewish liturgy—"your kingdom come on earth." The final utterance of the Book of Revelation is *Marana tha*, "Come quickly, Lord Jesus."[13] Thanksgiving is eschatological as well as a remembrance of things past.

Keeping in mind these four points about the earliest strata of Christian Eucharistic praying, let us examine the liturgical structure and themes of the earliest written text of a full Eucharistic prayer pattern. From the early third century, it is found in Hippolytus' *Apostolic Tradition*.[14] This text is not the only prayer pattern used in the early liturgy at Rome, but it has become important in research subsequent to its publication in the late nineteenth century and, more importantly, in ecumenical restoration of Eucharistic prayers in the twentieth century. It has become a paradigmatic model for nearly every major Christian body undertaking reform of its rites during the past twenty years.

After the presider and the assembled community share the ancient dialogue which concludes, "Let us give thanks to the Lord," "It is fitting and just (so to do)"; Hippolytus' account of the prayer continues:

> We give you thanks, O God,
> through your beloved servant, Jesus Christ.
> It is he whom you have sent
> in these last times
> to save us and redeem us,
> and be the messenger of your will.
> He is your Word,
> inseparable from you,
> through whom you made all things
> and in whom you take delight.
>
> You sent him from heaven
> into the Virgin's womb,
> where he was conceived, and took flesh.
> Born of the Holy Spirit and the Virgin,
> he was revealed as your Son.
>
> In the fulfillment of your will
> he stretched out his hands in suffering
> to release from suffering
> those who place their hope in you,
> and so he won for you a holy people.

After a brief section concerning Christ's passion and death and its power to "trample . . . the powers of hell" and the manifestation of the resurrection, the so-called "institutional narrative" is in-

**Don E. Saliers**

cluded. Reflecting all of the gospel accounts as well as the tradition which St. Paul had received orally (I Corinthians 11), this institutional narrative is also a command to "Do my *anamnesis*" or remembering:

> And so he took bread
> and gave you thanks, saying:
> Take, and eat:
> this is my body
> which will be broken for you.
> In the same way he took the cup, saying:
> This is my blood
> which will be shed for you.
> When you do this, you do it in memory of me.

This passage prescribes the ritual actions and is followed immediately by what is known technically as the anamnesis segment of the prayer: "Remembering therefore his death and resurrection, we offer you this bread and cup, thankful that you have counted us worthy to stand in your presence and show you priestly service." Here is the thankful response to what God has already given. Even in the recital of the "words of institution" there is thanksgiving, and again in the very act of presenting the bread and the cup in oblation. The language *and* the gesture of grateful response form an indissoluble unity.

The prayer then moves to invoke God's Holy Spirit upon the gifts offered and upon the whole people gathered; this is known in Greek as the *epiclesis* segment of the Eucharistic prayer:

> We entreat you to send your Holy Spirit
> upon the offering of the holy Church.
> Gather into one
> all who share in these sacred mysteries,
> filling them with the Holy Spirit
> and confirming their faith in the truth,
> that together we may praise you
> and give you glory
> through your Servant, Jesus Christ.

Especially noteworthy is the reappearance of the eschatological plea, "gather into one" the whole Church, with the implication of the whole human family and created order as well. The whole prayer then concludes with a great doxology: "All glory and honor is yours, Father and Son, with the Holy Spirit in the holy

Church, now and forever." To which the whole assembly shouts its "Amen"—let it be so!

PRAISE, THANKSGIVING, SUPPLICATION

In reflecting upon the whole structure of this prayer, we immediately see the rhythm of praise, thanksgiving, and supplication—all mediated christologically. The creation of the world is effected through Christ. This recalls the opening prologue of John's gospel wherein the Logos of God now made flesh is acknowledged as the same "word"—creative reason and power—by which all things were created, as well as the utterance of God in and through the prophets now "in the last days" incarnate. God is thanked and praised both for the holy acts in history and for the very glory of God's own life. The structure of the ancient Eucharistic prayer is again reminiscent of the heart of Jewish recitals found in such places as Psalm 136, in related canticles—"Song of the Three Young Men," for example—and in other liturgical prayers. God is praised and given thanks by recalling God's mighty works. The distinctive note of reciting the word and acts of Jesus Christ provides a personal element at the heart of Christian prayer. To "Do this"—eat the bread and drink the cup—is his anamnesis as well as a present experience of all that God has given in creation and redemption. This recital is not simply a recollection of a fixed point. Rather, it is akin to the form of remembrance at the Passover Seder. When the child asks the elders, "Why is this night different from all other nights?" the answer is given in the form of a narrative of the Exodus event. But it is clear also that on this *present* night—in this very prayer and ritual action of the meal—the reality of that *past* event is here and now, made actual among the community of memory and hope.

The pattern of thanksgiving in these early Eucharistic prayers shows a great range and depth. The act of gratitude makes present the founding events and the future as well. It is far more than outward ritual expression of inwardly felt gratitude. It is much more comprehensive than a simple recounting of one's blessings. Such a pattern of praise and thanksgiving contains both an invocation for the present activity of divine grace and a plea for the saving power of God signified in the descriptions and ascriptions of glory and mercy in God embedded in the prayed narrative. Such a remembering includes a hope for the future so that the

**Don E. Saliers**

thanks given and the praise rendered is directed toward God's future acts as well. In this way, the thanksgiving is radically eschatological in force.

At the same time we must note the sacrificial element of self-offering to God that is implicit in the text. This is the double function of the *anamnesis:* the worshippers offer bread and wine to God in solidarity with the self-giving of the life of Jesus. These gifts the community "offers" are possible only because they are first received as gifts from the hand of God to human beings. This exchange of gifts, then, is based upon the transformation of created material in and through the self-giving of God in creation and in human history. For the Christian community, all of this is concentrated in the way in which the life and deeds of Jesus Christ are like a parable of the whole creating and redemptive work of God. God's self-giving and the worshippers' symbolic self-giving at the table of the Eucharist embrace as the mystery at the heart of the Eucharistic action. A radical paradox emerges. Christ is both the celebrant and the one given and received. What he embodies is God's eternal self-giving to the world. What appears as "exclusivist" thanksgiving and praise is at the same time the most "inclusive" and universal praise. More than two centuries after Hippolytus wrote down the primitive Eucharistic liturgy, St. Augustine was to make the human consequences of this paradox explicit in his remark to the Christian community: "When you receive the Eucharist, it is your own mystery you receive."[15]

The *epiclesis* element mentioned above emphasizes the fact that it is the Holy Spirit of God who animates both the gifts presented and those who are "worthy to stand before" and to serve God. In other words, the full range of meanings in Christian thanksgiving must include acknowledgment of *both* mutuality between God and creation *and* the happy dependency of all things upon the grace of God. This is a "happy" or blessed dependency precisely because, in acknowledging with grateful hearts the creating and redeeming love of God and the life-giving Spirit, the human community fulfills its true nature: to praise and glorify God. The goal of human existence is reflected in liturgical terms by the first question and answer of the Westminster Shorter Catechism (1647–48): "What is the chief end of man?" Answer: "Man's chief end is to glorify God and to enjoy him for ever."

In these two crucial instances of the origin and early development of the great Eucharistic prayer at the heart of the central liturgy of the Christian faith, we have the most intensive and complex form of prayer and praying. To be formed in the language and gesture of this prayer is to acknowledge that all other forms of prayer and, indeed, all forms of contemplation and action are within the great parenthesis of praise and thanksgiving. So the concluding doxology reiterates the christological mediation of thanksgiving and supplication: "Through him glory to you and honor . . . now and for ever!"

### FURTHER IMPLICATIONS

This all-too-brief exposition of early Eucharistic prayers illustrates the four foundation points made earlier. We can now explore further ramifications of our initial thesis: at the heart of Christian liturgical prayer and action is a pattern of thanksgiving and praise which—when addressed to its most fitting object, the God of all creation—opens a way of life and consequently a way of knowing God. Such a knowing is not simply doctrinal or cognitive; it is profoundly affectional. Prayers must become *prayer;* liturgical actions must become ways of relating to God, to creation, and to other human beings. Otherwise, the full implications of prayer and liturgy are never understood. If other human emotions and intentions, no matter how virtuous or noble, are not brought to the praise and thanksgiving and glorification of God, they do not find their true source and unity. Such a thanksgiving, when coupled with its christological mediation in the Eucharist, can be commanded but not coerced. It requires communal ritual expression which forms the believers in the appropriate deep affections. Eucharistic praise is thus an intention-action pattern for human existence.

### PAIN: CHALLENGE TO GRATITUDE

One of the fundamental challenges to a life of gratitude is pain and suffering. This is especially true in Christian tradition because pain and suffering are not regarded as illusory but as historical and social realities. While the metaphysical views of other traditions diminish the problem of evil and suffering, the Christological mediation of the presence of God in creation and history heightens the problem. Unmitigated suffering counts against being grate-

**Don E. Saliers**

ful, and death seems to be the final enemy of gratitude. So how is it possible for Paul to command the emotion of joy in "Rejoice always" or to command the believers to "give thanks in all circumstances"?

The first point is that this is no naive joy or thanksgiving. Paul does not command us to follow a simple-minded maxim for human happiness. The liturgy itself does not call for rose-colored glasses through which we see that the world is not full of perplexities, pain, and sorrow, after all. On the contrary, Paul knows suffering in his own life—in his own physical body. The doxologies which punctuate his correspondence with the early Christian communities, particularly in Romans, are always seen against the background of the real vicissitudes of life. The praise and thanksgiving to God re-orients us to the essential relationships in life. One does not thank God for evil and suffering; rather, in the midst of suffering and perplexity one thanks and praises God for the gift of life and endurance. The thanking is itself an act of hope and resistance to what is evil—including the evil intentions and destructive desires which inhabit the human heart.

Here we must be cautioned against personal gratitudes which ignore the complexity of our social reality, including the social pathologies we have destructively internalized in our time: anxiety, self-imposed guilt, fear of neighbor and stranger, and terrors from a loveless and capricious moral world. Metz remarks on our tendency to be overly positive in the liturgy: because of an "absence of suffering in the official language of prayer," we "generally fail to notice what 'modern humanity' loses with the gradual impoverishment of the language of prayer."[16] What happens when *"eulogistic evasion of what really matters"* is our natural religious idiom?[17] We lose the only social language capable of expressing and sustaining our humanity in hope and love—therefore in true praise. Only to *appease* the individual conscience is to deny the trajectory, if not the essence, of biblically formed prayer. I have in mind the demanding emotional range of the psalms which do not shrink from what really matters. To pray either for or with those who are suffering or to pray out of our own suffering forces the liturgy to yield both its tremendous consolation and its depths of thanksgiving. Only here can we begin to discern and to acknowledge who this One is to whom we pray—the Lord who stretched out his arms on the cross to embrace all humankind.

**Teaching Us To Pray**

Here, liturgy can begin to form us in that gratitude and praise which can encompass all our griefs and all our joys.

In the second place, the Eucharistic prayer does not simply remember the "good things" or some Edenic, idealized past; rather, it remembers suffering and brokenness just at the most crucial point. Just as the memories of Israel recite that they were once in bondage to slavery in Egypt, so the Christian liturgy recalls bondage to sin and death and names the brokenness of turning aside. More to the point, however, is the fact that the Christological narrative recalls suffering and death in the very act of rendering thanks. The fact of pain and death is not avoided but recognized as part of the means by which redemption is brought about. In this sense, then, it is part of Christian gratitude to know the contrast between joy and suffering, between life and death, between moral evil and virtue. The vulnerability of the Christian tradition lies in the paradox of the extravagant claims made on behalf of a human life offered in radical obedience and full and thankful self-giving. Yet this is the crucial way in which pain, suffering, and death are remembered in the act of rendering God both *thanksgiving* for creation and redemption and *praise* for what is yet to be consummated for the whole cosmos. This is why Christian thanksgiving is not simple-minded or naive. This is also why it can never be merely interior, a state of mind or feeling. Thanksgiving must result in a way of living which is Eucharistic in character: giving thanks to God for who God is—in all circumstances, whether immediately good or ill. This admonition to be grateful and thankful is echoed in other Eucharistic prayers: "It is right . . . always and everywhere to give thanks to you, Holy God."

GRATITUDE, PRAISE, BEATITUDE

We have suggested that as faith and prayer mature in their experience of God and the world, simple gratitude for specific acts intermingles more and more with the glorification of God for God's own being in itself. In his *Reflections on the Psalms*, C. S. Lewis discusses his own struggle to understand why praise and thanks to God have been so central to the Christian tradition. He admitted that he was at first put off by the thought that God should demand this response. It distressed him that—in addition to gratitude, reverence, and obedience—he had to participate in a

**Don E. Saliers**

"perpetual eulogy." It seemed that God must be above such demands for gratification. He says later that he had overlooked the fact that all deep enjoyment overflows into praise unless it is deliberately prevented from doing so. This is simply a fact of human existence. Lovers praise their beloved, citizens their heroes and countries, and religious believers their saints. Moreover, he observed that the "most balanced and capacious minds praised most, while the cranks, misfits, and malcontents praised least."[18] He concludes that the psalmist's call for praise and thanksgiving was simply a call for what all healthy persons do when they address what they truly care about and revere. We delight to praise what we enjoy, Lewis remarks, "because the praise not merely expresses but completes the enjoyment; it is its appointed consummation."[19]

This is a corollary to the exchange of gifts at the heart of rituals of thanksgiving, which we saw at the heart of Eucharistic offering. Just as the gifts of bread and wine—first gratefully received as God's to give—are themselves offered in response, so the praise of God completes the enjoyment and delight in the acknowledgement of who God is and what human life becomes when "all things are referred to God."

Our understanding of gratitude and thanksgiving in the Christian tradition is incomplete without this intimate connection with praise. In all the great prayers of the Church, one finds this overflowing of thanksgiving into joy and praise. May we say that there is a mutuality of affective understanding here? A proper understanding of the object of true praise attunes our hearts and our minds to the gifts and the giver. In theological terms, to truly know God and neighbor is to love and to serve both precisely because, in worship, we come to understand the direction in which the mercy and compassion of God move—always toward the other. A full exploration of this point would lead to reflection on the inexhaustible glory and grace in the divine life. These qualities of God are never exhausted by our expressions of gratitude and praise because, even in God's self-giving to the world, the divine being remains veiled, inexhaustible, and not comprehensible to the human mind. Yet the prayer and liturgical traditions within Christianity form us in knowledge of the divine life as one of glory and grace. In the act of thanksgiving, we acknowledge gift and giver even though we cannot know the fullness of God.

**Teaching Us To Pray**

This leads us to an important connection between grace and gratitude which helps define the concept of human sin in the Christian tradition. We find one of the deepest insights into this connection in Karl Barth. "Grace and gratitude belong together like heaven and earth. Grace evokes gratitude like the voice an echo."[20] Barth's words imply that the failure or absence of gratitude in the creature is a transgression, a sin—whether voluntary or involuntary—against the creator. Failing to ascribe honor and glory to the divine being diminishes the human enterprise. Barth claims, "Radically and basically all sin is simply ingratitude— man's refusal of the one but necessary thing which is proper to and is required of him with whom God has graciously entered into covenant."[21]

This suggests that there are degrees of thankfulness in relationship to praise. The fullest praise in human life is reserved for the most worthy objects. Jonathan Edwards, among others, stressed the moral excellence and beauty of God as the supreme object of all holy affections. The more excellent and worthy the object of human reverence and delight, the more intense the praise and gratitude will be. This theme is found in many different forms in the Christian traditions, especially in the early theologians such as the Cappadocians. The modern writer, C. S. Lewis, links praise with beatitude in this remarkable sentence:

> If it were possible for a created soul fully . . . to 'appreciate,' that is to love and delight in, the worthiest object of all, and simultaneously at every moment to give this delight perfect expression, then that soul would be in supreme beatitude."[22]

This is the taproot of all elation and experienced joy in the religious life, as many traditions testify. There are moments in which sustained thanksgiving and praise allow us an experiential taste of bliss. In the Christian tradition, this is called an experience of the kingdom of God or the beatific vision. Such experiences in this life, however, are always partial, "through a glass darkly," and never fully allow us to behold the reality of God.

Even when the world is filled with death, we give thanks, for God's love endures forever as Psalm 136 sings. Bitterness, despair, and hopelessness are not part of God's intention, but they are human contrasting possibilities. To continue to acknowledge God in prayer in the midst of adversity as well as in good fortune is to

**Don E. Saliers**

understand more and more deeply who we are in light of who God is. Yet false and self-deceptive—self-congratulatory—forms of liturgy abound. Even these, however, cannot alter the central import of the most primary act of Christian life and prayer: to praise and thank God and to grow in gratitude as the mystery of human existence before God unfolds.

LITURGY AND LIFE

Authentic prayer is born of extremity and gratuitousness. Christian liturgical prayer, which from the beginning shaped prayer in solitude, is born in acknowledgement of life given by God in grace, that is, "without strings." Liturgy is also a rehearsal of the way we are to become related to one another and to the world. With respect to creation itself, one is brought to awe and wonder and gratitude when, suddenly, the familiar patterns of life are seen fresh. When the face or place encountered a hundred times before becomes luminous with what it is, there is gratitude. Gerard Manley Hopkins expressed this connection between liturgy and life well:

> Glory be to God for dappled things—
>   For skies of couple-colour as a brinded cow;
>     For rose-moles all in stipple upon trout that swim;
> Fresh-firecoal chestnut-falls; finches' wings'
>   Landscape plotted and pieced—fold, fallow, and plough;
>     And all trades, their gear and tackle and trim.
>
> All things counter, original, spare, strange;
>   Whatever is fickle, freckled (who knows how?)
>     With swift, slow; sweet, sour; adazzle, dim;
>
> He fathers-forth whose beauty is past change:
>     Praise him.[23]

Even greater than the sheer beauty of specific creatures—a rainbow, a sound, a bird in flight—is the sudden sense of the gratuitousness of all things. The wonder of being at all: this is the origin and the ever-refreshing source of gratitude in the human heart. Its power lies in the background of contrasts we have traced: light with dark, joy with sadness, the cup of water with thirst, the bread with hunger, life with death. The Eucharistic prayer contains contrast; a life of gratitude lived *in* God learns how to refer all these *to* God.

**Teaching Us To Pray**

We may regard Christian liturgy and its central prayer forms as an expression of the primordial gratuitousness of being. As communal prayer and ritual action, it also forms human capacities to receive the world as gift and to live thankfully within it. To recite the wonders of nature and history to the Source of all being, and to invoke the animating Power of all life is to learn gratitude as well as to express thanksgiving and praise.

Prayer, in both its Christian liturgical and personal-devotional dimensions, is, as Brother David Steindl-Rast has pointed out, a coming alive to gratuitousness.[24] It is the sustained prayerfulness over a long period of time which opens up the relationships between God and the world because it participates in the mutuality of gift, giver, and recipient. Giving thanks daily, which marked the early Christian community reported in Acts, finds its culmination and fullest sounding in the Eucharistic liturgy which is but a rehearsal of being Eucharistic in the world in relation to neighbor. Praying with the Church is a continual reminder and a training in the narratives and images which focus on God's self-giving as the primal gift—the primary sacrament. But such gratitude cannot be gained in a single episode. It is deep only because it moves toward the whole of life. It takes time to unfold in the passing circumstances of temporal existence. But it is a double journey—both into self-knowledge and into the mystery of God's own being and self-giving. Only a lifetime lived in prayerfulness and gratitude can grasp who God is, much less the mystery of God's self-disclosure in and through the pattern of a human life who is both celebrant and grace in the eucharist.

### GOD CALLS; GOD WAITS

A final cadence must be sounded. The liturgy can only teach us to pray because the triune life of God embraces us and calls the cosmos to its best being. The liturgy teaches us to become prayerful only because we continually cry out to the One who is present and celebrated, "Lord, teach us to pray." The liturgy can only teach us to pray because the life-giving Spirit invoked upon human persons, bread, wine, and water, continues to intercede for us with "sighs too deep for words."

Many go to church and attend worship who do not find themselves praying. Dialogue, mutuality, and communion with the living God are never guaranteed. But the mystery of Christian

**Don E. Saliers**

liturgy well celebrated remains; God is faithful and waits. So the liturgy in its whole range—from daily prayer to initiation rites to Eucharist to the burial of the dead—waits patiently for our humanity to be opened to it. The liturgy waits patiently like Scripture, like Jesus, like the whole life of God who, as Tolstoy once observed, "sees the truth but waits."

The greeting and singing, the reading, the telling, the praying, the offering, blessing, breaking, pouring out and the breaking, giving, and receiving always points beyond itself. Liturgy gathers us, carries us, and transfigures us into that which is not merely visible, audible, or sensible. Rather, liturgy carries us across the divide and prepares us for "what eye hath not seen, nor ear heard" yet which, Scripture says, has been prepared for those who love God. Those whom God loves—and that is all creatures great and small—are meant for this. Liturgy invites us to a "home where none of us has ever been."[25]

All liturgical gatherings, ferial or festive, simple or elaborate, plain or splendid, are pregnant with the future. Or, we might say, every liturgy is an act of resistance against *no* future, against hopeless, loveless, unjust, and faithless worlds. The oldest liturgical prayer, found both at the end of Scripture (Revelation 22:20) and in the *Dadache*, is but our beginning: "Come, Lord Jesus!" If Christian liturgy is to be the on-going prayer of Jesus Christ in and through his Body in the world, then all our human vulnerabilities and complexities and our primordial creaturely need to acknowledge the source and summit of human existence are brought to praise and thanksgiving "in, with, and through Jesus Christ in the unity of the Holy Spirit."

## NOTES

1. Johannes Metz and K. Rahner, *The Courage to Pray* (New York: Seabury, 1980) 9.
2. *Ibid.* 24.
3. Geoffrey Wainwright, *Doxology* (New York: Oxford University Press, 1980) 422.
4. David Steindl-Rast, *Gratefulness, the Heart of Prayer* (New York: Paulist Press, 1984) 40.

**Teaching Us To Pray**

5. Romano Guardini, *Prayer in Practice*, trns. by Prince Leopold of Lowenstein-Wertheim (New York: Pantheon Books, 1957) 96.

6. Guardini, *op. cit.* 98.

7. This point is often overlooked by those who treat the New Testament as a "rule-book" for worship. The liturgical context itself generated the literature. Doxological fragments throughout the Pauline letters, for example, and the very pattern of the Apocalypse of St. John are cases in point. A recent study which makes this point clearly is *Theology As Thanksgiving: From Israel's Psalms to the Church's Eucharist*, by Harvey H. Guthrie, Jr. (New York: Seabury, 1981).

8. Acts 2:42, 46 Revised Standard Version.

9. *Didache*, chapter 9, 1-4. Translation from *The Eucharist of the Early Christians*, by Willy Rordorf and others, trans. by Matthew J. O'Connell (New York: Pueblo Publishing Company, 1978) 2.

10. *Didache, op. cit.* 3.

11. See, for example, H. J. Gibbins, "The Problems of the Liturgical Section of the *Didache*,"*Journal of Theological Studies*, 36 (1935) 383–86.

12. A recent article of crucial import for a more technical understanding of the *Didache* is Thomas J. Talley's "The Eucharist Prayer of the Ancient Church According to Recent Research: Results and Reflections," *Studia Liturgica* 11 (1976) 138–57.

13. *Revelation* 22:20.

14. *Eucharistic Prayer of Hippolytus* (Washington: International Commission on English in the Liturgy, 1983). A few minor changes were made in this liturgical version published in *Holy Communion* (Nashville: Abingdon Press, 1987) 11.

15. St. Augustine, Sermon 272.

16. Metz, *op. cit.* 18.

17. Metz, *op. cit.* 20.

18. C. S. Lewis, *Reflections on the Psalms* (New York: Harcourt, Brace and World, 1958) 94.

19. *Ibid.* 95.

20. Karl Barth, *Church Dogmatics*, IV/1, (Edinburgh: T. and T. Clark, 1956) 41.

21. Karl Barth, *Church Dogmatics*, II/1 (Edinburgh: T. and T. Clark, 1957) 655.

22. C. S. Lewis, *The Weight of Glory and Other Addresses* (New York: Macmillan Publishing Company, 1949) 15.

**Don E. Saliers**

23. Gerard Manley Hopkins, "Pied Beauty" in *Poems of Gerard Manley Hopkins*, introduction by W. H. Gardner, third edition (New York and London: Oxford University Press, 1948) 74.

24. See his *Gratefulness, the Heart of Prayer, op. cit.*, chapter one.

25. See note 2.

Emilie Griffin

# The Challenge to Interiority

Let me state my thesis very simply from the beginning: *the challenge to Christian interiority is a challenge first and foremost to the imagination.* And to the extent that we as Christians have failed to pray well, we have failed to imagine well these important points:

> the possibilities of prayer
> the power of prayer
> the surrender of prayer
> the necessity of prayer
> the richness of prayer
> the treasure of prayer
> the political might of prayer
> the social breadth of prayer
> the unifying strength of prayer
> the power of prayer to forge new relationships in the spirit
> the world-embracing nature of prayer.

Let me say it again: *the deepest challenge to Christian interiority in our time and in our culture is a challenge to the imagination.*

When prayer fails us, it is because our imagination fails us. It is our imagination which has failed to bring forward from the past the possibility and option of deeply *contemplative* prayer. Imagination fails us when it fails to bring forward from the past the *liturgical* understanding of prayer which was present in the earliest Church and which is present in the renewal of Vatican II.

Our imagination has failed us because we have failed to image prayer, not only for our contemporaries but even for ourselves, as

**Challenge to Interiority**

the deepest yearning of the human heart, the gift of the self
which must be made daily, the way into a deeper understanding
of God, the way out of a thousand ancient and modern dilemmas
from drug dependency, to alcoholism, to violence, to war.

Our imagination has failed us, or we have failed it. But the solution is within our grasp. We can imagine prayer, and we can
pray.

Together, let us consider five related questions that can help us
to understand the contemporary dilemmas of Christian interiority.

> Question 1 How does our culture discourage Christian
> prayer?
>
> Question 2 What does contemplative prayer require of us?
>
> Question 3 How do we experience the transforming power
> of contemplation? How does it happen? What
> must we do, or not do, in order to be trans-
> formed?
>
> Question 4 Does contemplation have anything to do with
> the public prayer of the Church, that is, with
> liturgy?
>
> Question 5 What is the relationship of prayer both to the
> apostolate and to the daily life and mission of
> the Christian?

We will consider these questions one by one. As we do so, let
us form for ourselves an image of Christian contemplatives. Who
are they? Where do they live and work? How do they spend their
time? Where do they worship God? How do they pray? What
other people do they pray with and for? And more importantly, in
what universe or multiple universes do they dwell?

First, let me say that I believe that Christian contemplatives
dwell in three universes and only three, and these are their places
of ordinary habitation. They dwell, first and foremost and always,
in the *wilderness*. The rocks, sand, twigs, and wildflowers of the
wilderness are not alien to them. There in the wilderness they
hear their Lord speaking. There in the wilderness, they hear the
poor crying. There, they see John the Baptist going before them in
a loincloth, feasting on wild locusts and honey. There in the
wilderness they are afraid, lost, and doubtful. And there in the
wilderness they find their Lord.

Second, these contemplatives of ours dwell also in *Church*. They

**Emilie Griffin**

are quilted into the fabric of it; they are threaded through it like a silver needle; they are patchwork persons, part of the whole design. The Church is so much a part of them that they are never far from it, wherever they are. They have been grafted on to it by baptism. They are twigs on the branch of the vine. They are a ragged fringe on the torn cloth of the garment which ought to be seamless. These contemplatives of ours go as beggars and pilgrims into every household on their way, and when they go in, they bring the Church with them. It is under their skins.

Third, our contemplatives dwell in the *marketplace*. There they find such diversity of experience that they can hardly take it in. The marketplace is as broad as the world itself, and a rich diversity of cultures and nations is represented there. There is Byzantine lore and Greek philosophy, Hebrew wisdom and Arab calculation, French fragrance and Russian roulette, Latin culture and American resourcefulness. Every race and nation is represented, every cultural hope and national identity, every prayer-style, every heritage, every form of religious experience, every fruit of the weather and the soil—everything, in short, that the rains, the earth, and the mind of humankind can fashion. All these attractions, competing for attention and predominance, engage the mind and spirit of our contemplatives in action, and among them they must choose, must create, must discern, must ultimately decree or decry. These are the people who stand for us. They represent the Lady Contemplation. Keep her in mind as we go on pilgrimage for the city of perfection, the Zion of resolution and peace.

THE INFLUENCE OF CULTURE

I turn now to the first question: *how does our culture discourage Christian prayer?* As we consider this question, we are also considering a central thesis: the challenge to Christian interiority can be measured in terms of our failure to imagine prayer.

And the answer is simple; we don't have far to look!

1. Our culture challenges Christian interiority with a language and a philosophy of achievement which allows no time for prayer and service to God.
2. Our culture challenges interiority by a success-oriented mentality and a mentality of sophistication which refuses to take God at his word.

**Challenge to Interiority**

3. Our culture challenges interiority by a success-driven concept of space and time.
4. Our culture challenges interiority by what it values: By valuing exteriority, the material, the external, the outer values over the inner values of charity and peace.
5. Our culture challenges interiority by stereotyping prayer as rote performance and lip service.
6. Our culture challenges interiority by failing to model prayer as a life-style, by failing to show in its own behavior the witness and the example of what praying people might be and might become.

This same world-driven, success-driven mentality which threatens contemplation threatens liturgical prayer as well. Both are, to a success-oriented culture, a waste of time. In the world's view of the right use of time, prayer is time wasted. Within this frame of mind, both Eucharist and contemplation must suffer from the same exclusionary prejudice. Both kinds of worship are step-children in a universe of hard-nosed achievement and practicality where we are programmed to achieve. Our scheme of values demands it. A phrase of Kipling's—"the unforgiving minute"—says it well. In his poem "If"—which once was taught to children to form good conduct—he sets up the relentless ideal. Our duty lies in filling that unforgiving minute with sixty seconds worth of distance run; then, the earth and all that is in it will be ours.

Is the Church as *institution* a stranger to this success mentality? Far from it. I am sorry to say, society's attitudes are by no means external to the Church. The Church is power driven, as society is, by time-frames, time lines, and relentless goals. Anyone who has worked in any institutional enterprise—whether it be the office of education or the social apostolate—can testify that the workload proliferates; the stacks of envelopes mount; the stuffing, sorting, and postage metering builds up in almost geometric progression. There is always more to do tomorrow than could have been conceived of yesterday. Machines and people are subject to burnout; strategies, agendas, hearts, even photocopy machines go up in flames. The Church *as institution* scorns prayer when it isn't geared to some specific purpose. We are always—in every endeavor—wanting to know what's in it for us and how we can best play the angles toward specific, success-driven goals.

**Emilie Griffin**

I am only saying that the Church is human. And whatever her divine prerogatives, she often sides with the world where achievement is concerned. Holy Mother Church, whatever her feminine side, has some trouble with surrender. She is sometimes hard as a rock when she wants to have it her way.

### REQUIREMENTS OF CONTEMPLATIVE PRAYER

The answer to the second question, *What does contemplative prayer require of us?*, is a reversal, a turning away from the success motive. It demands the yielding, the surrender that the Gospel speaks about.

First, contemplative prayer demands that we recognize that we are powerless, that half measures avail us nothing. We must surrender ourselves entirely to God's protection and care. Seeking success is useless. Instead, what we need to do is surrender.

Second, we must let go of our delusions about self, about space, about time:

- timeboundedness that says we don't have time to pray.
- low self-esteem that says, "God talks to other people, not to me."
- lack of faith that says, "Nothing will happen if I pray."
- arrogance that says, "Everything else I am doing for God is a sufficient offering; therefore, I don't need to pray."

Third, most of all we must let go of fear:

- fear that prayer will change us
- fear that God will ask something of us which is beyond our powers
- fear of receiving a call and a mission
- fear of our own inadequacy to respond to such a call

As every praying Christian knows, our fears are well founded. We are all afraid of the call to follow in the footsteps of Jesus Christ. Our fear is Peter's fear. We are afraid that when the time comes we will say, "I never knew the man. Is he a Galilean? I was never in Galilee."

The yielding, the surrender that is asked of us is the essence and foundation of Christian prayer—of any prayer—whether we call it contemplative or not. It is the willingness to say, "We are not enough for ourselves, by ourselves." It is willingness to bend the knee and say, "My Lord and My God."

**Challenge to Interiority**

This kind of surrender exists only in practice. It is never theoretical. One cannot surrender in the abstract. Surrender is always concrete. We must surrender in the flesh, with our whole selves—heart, head, hands, and all. There is no holding back, and there is no other way. I am not speaking now of technique, of specific phrases and mantras, of a way of prayer that can be practiced and mastered as a lifestyle, a form of mastery and control. Far from it. For there is no way to master surrender. To yield is to give way, to let down, to drop down, to be nothing but what God wills us to be, to unmaster, to unloose, to undo, to be clay in the potter's hands.

I am speaking now of an inner dialogue, a meeting, a confrontation—that takes place nowhere and everywhere—in the inaccessible reaches of the heart. It is a power struggle, a wrestling—Jacob's wrestling with the angel on the road. In one sense, it is never complete because it is always ongoing. The surrender once made in our baptism or when we first chose the Lord must be made over and over again. The prodigal son comes home again and again and again. Newman, in his sermon on Christian repentance, says, "The most perfect Christian is ever but beginning. . . ." and comes home again like the prodigal to be tried over and over again.

### TRANSFORMING POWER

Now for the third question: *What of the transforming power of contemplation? Is it overrated? Is it a reality? And what if anything do we mortals have to do with it?*

When we speak of the transforming power of contemplation someone always has a tendency to yawn or guffaw. Who are these people who come to us speaking about myths and miracles? What planet did they fall from? What tornado brought them here? The transforming power of contemplation sounds like heady stuff, hyperbole. The fact, however, is that prayer changes us in ways that are difficult to quantify.

"How has prayer changed you?" comes the glib question from the talk-show host, and the guests, however prayerful they may be, become suddenly tongue tied.

"Mention five or six ways that prayer has changed you so that our studio audience and our listeners at home can identify with your experience and keep those telephones ringing," he insists.

**Emilie Griffin**

The guests are stammering, inarticulate.

Finally, one of them says, cautiously, ''Well, I've set a higher priority on family life. My marriage is holding together. I'm willing to make compromises I didn't used to make. Also, my self-esteem is higher. I am learning how to say 'no.''

Tame stuff, this. What the person doesn't say is, ''I was drinking to excess and neglecting my children. The Lord gave me the strength to walk away from alcohol,'' or ''I was consumed by anger and self-pity. I found little ways to pick on my husband and children as an outlet for those feelings. Now I've stopped doing that, by the grace of God.''

''I'm beginning to be able to see into other people's hearts. When they hate me, I can feel it. I just know.'' But the person doesn't say that.

''But behind the hate I can see something else—the hurt that is buried deep in their hearts. I can see that the hate is not really because of me but because of some way they've been hurt before.'' She doesn't say that.

It is difficult to speak about the transforming power of contemplation because it sounds outrageous, arrogant, self serving. When asked about the transforming effect of contemplation upon ourselves, we find it impossible to testify. But Isaiah II tells us all about the ways the Spirit will change us. We also read about it in Galatians 5. The transforming effect of the Spirit brings change reflected in action: love, gentleness, long-suffering, patience, forbearance, temperance, self-control.

But people of prayer cannot testify to these things. To do so would be self-serving. Instead, they have to testify to the way the world looks from the vantage point of the one who prays. Is there one way of describing that subjective viewpoint, that look through the lens of the praying eye? One simple word says it: transparency. Transparency is one of the effects of prayer seen from the point of view of the one who prays. It is that growing clarity which happens, almost in spite of ourselves, the more we give ourselves to prayer. It is a kind of immediacy, an insight, a sense of being able to enter into things and into experience more deeply in a way we could never have fully anticipated. It is a grasping of existence itself, a possessing it in an unaccountably different way. Yet it is not a peak experience in the sense of being at the heights.

**Challenge to Interiority**

Instead, it is a sense that day-to-day existence, events, persons, actions, things that are already ours, are more nearly ours than before—more open, more available to our understanding. Transparency is not light or illumination, but it is akin to both of them. It is a seeing through the veil. It is an experience of going beyond ourselves and our limitations while at the same time being conscious of the definition of ourselves. We see our boundaries and at the same time we see beyond them. Contemplation frees us to do this in ways we do not understand.

Now we grasp reality not by an effort to master circumstance but instead by a full admission that we are powerless, that we are unable to control or comprehend events.

The more we admit what we are and are not, the more we come to know how little we can accomplish and control and how inadequate our formulas are; the more we encounter the edges of the world falling away from us—the ships, once seen at a distance, now disappearing over the rim of the world—the more we know the arc of our own vision; and the more we are conscious of the boundedness of our experience, the more, by a paradox and mystery, we see.

The universe and everything in it is made known to us, given to us by God, lit up from within. And the more this happens, the more we sense the wonder: *God is for us what we could not be for ourselves. The more we accept our blindness the farther we can see.*

Sometimes this experience of transparency comes through particularity. This one moment happening now, this rainstorm in which I am being drenched, this feeling of mushiness in my shoes, this joke, these tears, the dampness of this air, this Caladium plant with the deep red leaves, this *thisness*, is a glimpse of the real.

God is not everywhere, not in heaven; instead, he is in this moment and I am there with him. And this experience of God in the particular, God in the person, God in the event, is everything that I am and everything God is in a single glimpse. A leaf, the root of a tree, the dimeness of a dime glinting in the palm of my hand, this very dime, no other, thisness floods us with conclusiveness. Instant on instant, one event following another, is Yahweh saying, I am.

Sometimes this transparency gives us the capacity to read hearts, to know the thoughts of others—even their hatreds—

**Emilie Griffin**

90

without being told, not only from their eyes and body language but by some immediacy of vision, some seeing that is pure gift, not from anything we do. This transparent seeing lets us love the ones who hate us, the ones we also have provocation to hate.

In the comprehension of our seeing, we go past the outer image of the person to the inner image created by God, an identity imperfectly seen perhaps, but plain enough to compel our charity and our love. This transparent seeing does not happen only when we are praying. It goes with us into the rest of life, a residue of prayer.

This change in ourselves also lets us see Christ in the pain of events; in the distress and despair of others; in the homeless drifters, their faces and bodies ravaged by destitution and alcohol. Because of transparency, we can love them, we can experience their pain. We can be moved towards them to help, to attend, to do for them what we can, to take them generously into our prayer. Transparency means we can feel our identity with those in need. It is what moves us to say "I love you" to the panhandler who meets us on the street and begs from us what little we have to spare.

This comprehension lets us confront our own defeats. It lets us distance ourselves from our own anxiety and call it by its rightful name. This is the seeing that lets us walk ahead on a path that is not plain, where the destination is hidden, but with a constant sense that God himself is both at the destination and on the way.

Because of transparency, we come to understand our own yearning. We start to accept it, to be shaped by it, to know that yearning as a constant of our existence. This yearning is the mark and reminder of God. It is his mark on us. To accept the yearning is to shoulder the yoke, the unfreedom that will make us free.

Transparency opens up a passage into the fullness that makes us want to fast. We understand at last that not tasting is better than tasting, closer to the sum and substance of reality. It is a comprehension of the falsity of sampling experience as a way to fulfillment. Now we even begin to question the idea of fulfillment; we sense there is more to life than being fulfilled. We begin to believe that doing without—the emptiness that makes itself empty for God—is a deeper experience of truth than the constant plunging into things only to say we have done so.

Transparency moves us close to some experiences, but may

**Challenge to Interiority**

separate us sharply from others. We may distance ourselves from those conversations with people that are about what we did, where we've been, who we know, what we own. Transparency opens up a kingdom but closes other doors with a bang. Because we now see some life styles crumbling to ashes before our very eyes, it is harder to dialogue with those who live by things.

Transparency is the clarity that knows less is more, the realization that we don't need to carve our mark on existence so much as we need to let it carve its mark on us.

Chastity, continence, mildness, modesty, patience, longanimity—all these flow spontaneously from the clarity of vision given to us. Even sorrow and pain may call us to a contemplation of Christ, for within the events, we can see him at work transforming the monstrous observable facts into an image of himself. This happens not because we think it but because we live it out by prayer that puts us into the heart of things as they really are.

What happens to people who pray?

If they are willing to be transformed, God will transform them. But this happens not all at once but invisibly, by degrees. Gradually, their inner lives take hold; slowly, their outer lives change. They may live in the same city, hold the same job, attend the same church, frequent the same places, attend the same business meetings. But their hearts lie in the inner life, and they are moved by that. In a sense, they are part of an underground. They don't mention how prayer has changed them. Perhaps they don't even know. If anyone asks them about it, they are embarrassed and change the subject as soon as they can.

CONTEMPLATION AND LITURGICAL PRAYER

The fourth question asks us: *what does contemplation have to do with the liturgical prayer of the Church, with public prayer?* To answer this question, we must remember our contemplatives who live at one and the same time in three spheres—the wilderness, the church, and the marketplace.

Because they learned their prayers before Vatican II, one of their early styles of contemplation was adoration of the Blessed Sacrament. It was their custom to wait breathlessly for the ringing of the bells and the elevation of the host. Summoned to this moment by ear and eye, their hearts stirred at the sudden presence of the

**Emilie Griffin**

Lord in the midst of his people. They knew, always, that at Mass they could pray the prayer of simple regard. We look at him, they thought, and he looks at us.

But now they are twenty-five years older. Our contemplatives have learned new ways to pray. The windows of the Church have been flung open, and winds of change—liturgical and contemplative—have brought new ways of worship and new styles of prayer to enrich and to refresh. What is the relationship *now* between contemplation and liturgical prayer? Now, our contemplatives can see their Lord imaged not only in the sacred host, not only in statuary and stained glass, but also in the sacred word-imagery of Eucharistic prayer.

> Calling to mind the death your Son endured for our salvation,
> his glorious resurrection and ascension into heaven . . .
> . . . the Victim whose death has reconciled us to yourself . . .
> . . . a man like us in all things but sin . . .
> . . . in him a new age has dawned,
> the long reign of sin has ended,
> a broken world has been renewed,
> and man is once again made whole . . .
> . . . the word through whom you made the universe,
> the savior you sent to redeem us . . .
> . . . for our sake he opened his arms on the cross,
> he put an end to death
> and revealed the resurrection . . .

Not only in these images of Jesus as Savior but also in the images of his holy people it is possible to contemplate the Lord, to be passionately united with him:

> . . . from age to age you gather a people to yourself . . .
> . . . strengthen in faith and love your pilgrim Church on earth . . .
> Father, hear the prayers of the family you have gathered . . .
> . . . the fellowship of your apostles and martyrs,
> John the Baptist, Stephen, Matthias, Barnabas,
> and all the saints . . .

And in blazing images of angels and archangels, in transcendent imagery of a God beyond images, here, too, the contemplative heart is set on fire:

> Father in heaven, it is right that we
> should give you thanks and glory;

**Challenge to Interiority**

93

you are the one God, living and true.
Through all eternity you live in
unapproachable light.
Source of life and goodness
You have created all things
To fill your creatures with every blessing
and lead all to the joyful vision of your light.
Countless hosts of angels stand before you
to do your will;
they look upon your splendor
and praise you, night and day.
United with them, and in the name
of every creature under heaven,
we too praise your glory as we sing.
"Holy, Holy, Holy, Lord,
God of power and might.
Heaven and Earth are filled with your glory.
Hosanna in the Highest.
Blessed is He who comes in the name of the Lord.
Hosanna in the Highest."

To the extent that we give ourselves to the Lord in contemplation whenever we are at Mass, we are open to experiencing the reality of the communion of saints. We are being bound to one another in fellowship by cords of pure spiritual friendship, grappled together—as Shakespeare says—with hoops of steel.

CONTEMPLATION AND THE APOSTOLATE

The fifth and final question asks us: *What is the relationship of contemplation to the apostolate: the daily life and mission of the Christian?* In a sense, this question has been partially answered by what we have already said.

Let me only add that I believe the more we love the Lord, the closer we come to him in authentic prayer, the more we taste and feel him as part of our own lives and are cherished by his tenderness and passionate love, the more intensely we will be moved to care for and comfort his people, to minister to his flock, to bind up the wounds of his people, to feed his sheep.

I have often heard the fear expressed that people who pray will end up by walling themselves away from experience, turning deaf ears to the needs of those around them, being false to the hungers and demands of the poor and powerless.

**Emilie Griffin**

94

In practice, I do not know of one instance where this has been true. Occasionally, I meet a poor soul so clinging to her own mystical experiences of the Lord that she cannot break free of them to mind any other store, to mend any other garment, or bind anyone else's wounds. So random and so infrequent is this experience that I find it hard to call it a trend.

Moreover, such people are themselves the handicapped, the needy to whom we must minister. It is for us, who understand prayer as a call to action and ministry, to open the ears of the deaf and raise the halt and the lame. Contemplation is not isolation. Contemplation is seeing the Lord with the eye of prayer and with a heart filled with love, and this visionary experience is freeing, world seeking, world loving, world embracing. Pierced with the sword of Christ, our hearts are open to Christ, open to the needs of his people and his world. The walls of our very selves are violated, and we are vulnerable to every cry of hunger and despair. Yes, we are afraid. Our violated, vulnerable hearts are nevertheless capable of courage. We march without boots, without shoes, on pilgrim feet into a country of possibilities, still raising the tattered flag of expectation.

> Lord Jesus, Seigneur,
> You of the Sacred Heart,
> As you bled for the world we will also bleed;
> As you died for us we will also die.
> And more than that,
> more than dying for your people
> in far off places
> in unknown spaces,
> here,
> in the midst of our middle class
> existence,
> in the mudslide of our
> ordinary lives,
> we will live for your people
> and be generous to them
> as you give us the grace
> and the light and the power
> to do it.

I now return to my thesis that *the challenge to Christian interiority is first and foremost a challenge to the imagination.*

**Challenge to Interiority**

I want to embroider that just a bit. I simply mean that contemporary persons need imagination even to conceive of the possibility of prayer. So weakened are we, so impoverished in our understanding of prayer, that we can hardly see beyond our noses. For many of us, prayer is still a matter of asking for things, still mostly a plea for favors.

To experience the banquet of contemplation, the feast in the liturgy or outside of it, we have to imagine a God who loves us, who prepared a place for us, who spread the table with many good things, who wants us to come to the table and sup with him.

It is only when we imagine this Lord who has spread the table for us, this Lord who invites us to feast with him, this Church in which he gathers his intimate friends, only then can we open our lips to taste the rich delights of worship. Imagination is the key to the garden of liturgical and contemplative prayer.

But imagination can do more. Imagination can also help us to discern the invisible connections between our liturgy, our contemplation, and our apostolate to the world. These connections are not new connections, yet they are strange to us. They have been covered over by centuries of disuse and neglect. They are rusted out, corroded; we have to dip them in some new liquid in order to burnish them again. This restoration helps us begin to see that the structure of our liturgy is able to link together all the desires of our hearts:

> Our desire for prayer in private,
> Our desire for prayer in common,
> Our desire for liturgical worship, both formal and informal,
> Our desire to be instruments of change and transformation in the world.

For in and through the liturgy, we can see a structure and design wherein the whole Church is in harmony with the Church within the world. Through it, we can glimpse a colorful sequence of moods and moments: the purple of repentance, the blue of contemplation, the scarlet of surrender. We can wear the green of ordinary time, put on the white of special feasts, don the rose-red garments of rejoicing.

Through the imagery of the liturgy, we can imagine a world at peace, a world rich with possibilities and flowering with hope. All

**Emilie Griffin**

these moods and moments are possible to persons of prayer when they unite their prayers to the prayer of the Church and pray for the sake of the world. But to tap these resources there must be discipline. There is no substitute for structure. The structures of liturgy remain our best hope for a unified Church, a Church renewed and renewing the world, refreshing us from the deepest wells of holiness. For the person of authentic prayer, there is no greater value than structure and discipline.

I am speaking now not only of the discipline that is provided by liturgical design. I am also speaking of the way that an individual rule of life can be pieced together by the prayerful Christian from the traditions of the Church and stitched into a garment that has about it all the simplicity and comfort of an apron or a smock— pockets filled with scraps of poetry and prayer-cards, stuffed with Bible verse Scripture cookies and Scripture teabags, yet always reflecting the prayerful priorities of a long tradition, shaped by a heritage centuries old, and reaching forward into the future in hope.

However silly such contemplatives may seem puttering among their prayer-petunias, they are even so grafted into the body of Christ. There are gardens in their faces where lilies and sweet roses blow. For them, liturgical worship links their contemplation with the world-wide vision of the Church: dreams of a world at peace, of nations living in harmony, of a Jerusalem that is not yet. And the inward energy of their prayers carries them forward daily toward ministry, toward concern for neighbor, toward compassionate giving.

One foot in the dirt, one foot in the bayou, one hand on the Bible, and one hand on the cross, they cut a funny figure, all right. But their eyes are on the crucified Lord. And beyond him, they can see the stars. There is no doubt that faithfully praying Christians want to pray in harmony with the whole Church, their hearts beating with the Church, with the heart of Christ in the Church. And they see in the Church a structure and a discipline—not only the discipline of liturgy but also the discipline of a rule of life, imposing as it does a life-commitment and making available all the riches of prayer-wisdom which the Church makes available to her faithful ones.

This structure and discipline is a source of power and vitality for them, one which empowers them as leaders and shapers of

**Challenge to Interiority**

values, forces for good in society, communicators and role models, planners and ministers.

The liturgy, then, is the linchpin of a renewed structure for Christian prayer. For it is liturgy that coordinates our private prayer with our public prayer and leads us toward a commitment in and for the world.

*Imagination is the heart of it all*, but not imagination running wild like fire in the stubble. Rather, it is imagination as an energy source for a renewed experience of a praying Church, a worshipping Church, a Church praying and working in the world and for the sake of the world.

Imagination is hope. For by imagining prayer, we imagine ourselves at prayer; by imagining ourselves in the presence of God, we are in his presence; by imagining ourselves at the service of our neighbor, we become more open to the possibility of loving Christ in our neighbors, near or far.

By this mysterious interconnection of contemplation, worship, and discipleship, we marshal resources of the spirit; we become soldiers of surrender for the overcoming of the world.


John F. Baldovin, S.J.

# The Liturgical Year: Calendar for a Just Community

> *Then at last will all creation be one.*
> *And we shall join in singing your praise*
> *Through Jesus Christ our Lord.*
> Eucharistic Prayer A

Then I saw a new heaven and a new earth; for the first heaven and the first earth had passed away, and the sea was no more. And I saw the holy city, a new Jersualem, coming down out of heaven from God, prepared as a bride for her husband; and I heard a great voice from the throne saying: "Behold the dwelling of God is with human beings. God will dwell with them, and they shall be God's people, and God will be with them. God will wipe away every tear from their eyes, and death shall be no more, neither shall there be

**John F. Baldovin,** S.J.

98

any mourning nor crying nor pain any more, for the former things have passed away" (Rev 21:1-4).

These two visions, the first from the International Commission on English in the Liturgy's experimental Eucharistic Prayer A and the second from the Book of Revelation, sum up in a marvelous way the extraordinary Christian vision of the world as a place of reconciliation, freedom, healing, justice and Shalom, God's peace. It is the Christian vision of the kingdom, the reign of God.

In the face of the privatization of religion in our own culture, we are beginning to realize increasingly that the Christian vision of the fullness of the end times—the eschatological vision—is intrinsically social or communal. No Christian community, which means no worshipping community, can afford any longer to stick its corporate head in the sand of individualistic salvation at the expense of concerns about society and the culture at large. Therefore, it is imperative that all people who are responsible for the Church's liturgy—and this means in the last analysis the whole worshipping community but especially those charged, whether ordained or not, with special responsibility for the Church's worship—must seek out ways for Christian worship to reflect a response to the contemporary world.

Before dealing with this question in terms of the liturgical calendar, it is necessary to clarify the biblical meaning of divine justice which must be the source of all Christian efforts. The Christian vision of divine justice is of a justice that transcends every political and economic system. Two of the parables of Jesus illustrate this important point. The first is the parable of the Prodigal Son or, better, the Merciful Father (Luke 15:11-32). One misses a vital aspect of this story if one confines its interpretation merely to the forgiveness and reconciliation of the individual sinner with God, for in it there is a message about divine justice. God does not require retribution of the wayward son, but rather conversion. Moreover, unlike an ordinary oriental patriarch, God becomes a fool by letting go of all the trappings of prestige to greet the wayward one and provide him with the very best. There is even more to the story, for at the end, a sobering and at the same time liberating point is made with regard to the elder son who is angered at the Father's profligacy. The elder son is called upon to recognize the depths of his own unrighteousness or injustice, and the listener is put in the place of that son. The parable is incomplete

**Calendar for a Just Community**

and calls for the response of the listeners; we are called upon to complete the story by our own response to the foolishness of divine justice.

The second parable may be even more disturbing to the normal, everyday, common-sense approach to a just world. It is Matthew's parable of the workers in the vineyard (Mt. 20:1-16). Here, the usual pay scale is turned topsy-turvy when the owner of the vineyard in his lavish generosity pays the same amount to those who have worked for an hour as to those who have worked all day. To be sure, the main point of the parable is not about social justice but rather God's election. However, the story is offensive to our normal sense of what is just. What seems unjust by human standards pales before the abundance of divine goodness, a compassion that relativizes all human attempts to be just.

These brief reflections on only two of the parables need to be complemented by other images in the message of Jesus—for example, the last-judgment scene in Matthew 25:31-46 where salvation hinges on one's response to those in need or Jesus' own ministry of liberation in Luke 4:16-30. The transcendence of divine justice cannot absolve us of the divine challenge to cooperate in the building of a just society by every available means, but it can serve as a warning that no political or social scheme is ultimate. The final realization of justice and peace will outdo all of our best efforts, but the call to Christian social justice demands both a fidelity to the biblical notion of justice and to the Christian tradition of working out that justice in diverse cultural situations and historical periods. The U.S. Catholic Bishops' Pastoral, *Economic Justice for All*, puts it this way:

> Our reflection on U.S. economic life today must be rooted in this biblical vision of the kingdom and discipleship, but it must also be shaped by the rich and complex tradition of Catholic life and thought. Throughout its history the Christian community has listened to the words of Scripture and sought to enact them in the midst of daily life in very different historical and cultural contexts.[1]

The incarnation of that vision in terms of the liturgical calendar's feasts and seasons is our concern here, for the Christian vision is normally reflected by the worship of the Church. To quote *Economic Justice for All* once again:

> Challenging U.S. economic life with the Christian vision calls for a deeper awareness of the integral connection between worship and

**John F. Baldovin**, S.J.

the world of work. Worship and common prayers are the well-springs that give life to any reflection on economic problems and that continually call the participants to greater fidelity and discipleship.[2]

It must be added that in the ongoing Sunday assembly Christians are formed by a liturgical cycle that must have political and economic consequences if those same Christians are to offer credible and authentic witness in the contemporary world. To arrive at some answers to the question, "How can the liturgical calendar aid us in manifesting the Christian vision of peace and justice?"— the third part of this essay—one should ask two questions beforehand: What is there about contemporary culture and therefore contemporary liturgical life that conflicts with this vision in general? and How have liturgical calendars shaped communal Christian belief and action in the past?

I. INDIVIDUALISM, COMMUNITY, AND THE CALENDAR

The liturgical calendar of the Roman Catholic Church and other mainline Christian Churches is indeed problematic today, for it presupposes in many ways a social and cultural world that no longer exists. Recently, James Sanders has criticized the Church lectionary and calendar: "Most of the festivals in the Christian calendar are but ancient agricultural and fertility-cult seasonal celebrations, barely Christianized."[3]

There is some truth to this charge, but what the author fails to understand is that the Christians of the ancient Mediterranean world had little choice but to adapt their celebrations to the culture in which they lived—at least to the extent that Christianity was congruent with those cultures. The alternative was to become a small sectarian group, lamenting the ways of the world. Moreover, as Thomas Talley has recently shown, the origins of the various Christian feasts and seasons were far more complex than the mere adaptation of agricultural or pagan festivals. There was inevitably some adaptation to cultural conditions: as an example, the cooptation of the Roman festival of the dead—*cara cognatio* on February twenty-second—as the feast of the Chair of St. Peter. One must note that we have a tendency to argue for inculturation in the contemporary world while scorning it in the past. Such myopia will not serve us well in discerning how the liturgical year can be a vehicle for social justice.

**Calendar for a Just Community**

But back to the problem at hand: the liturgical year and our own socio-cultural calendars do not match. It is extremely difficult for the liturgical year to mold people's everyday experience. The problem is much deeper than the calendar. We live in a world—at least this is true of assimilated, English-speaking North Americans—where a basic, gut-level commitment to common values and a common world view has broken down. Such a world has a great deal of trouble focusing on common symbols; this in turn hurts the liturgy which is rooted in the celebration of such symbols in ritual action. In other words, liturgy requires a passionate, even if implicit, commitment to a common view of the world. This does not imply that every liturgical experience is exclusively communal; there are times when individuals experience something completely different from the rest of the community depending on their mood or circumstances. However, today's problem is that we tend to bring fundamentally individualized experiences and expectations to liturgical life.

This fact has been well borne out by Mark Searle's essay in this collection as well as by other contributions to recent sociological literature. I will mention two examples. In *The Fall of Public Man*, Richard Sennett demonstrates the gradual individualization of Western people from the eighteenth century to the present.[4] In *Habits of the Heart*—case studies of individuals from different walks of life—Robert Bellah and his colleagues, in even more striking fashion, show how fragmented our contemporary American culture really is.[5] In terms of religion, it seems that the individuals who were subjects of the study are representative of Americans seeking personal experiences in the midst of their life's journey. Put simply, they have engaged in common worship for therapeutic purposes. It is difficult to step outside this scenario because the therapeutic life is as common as the air we breathe, as real to us as angels and demons were to our forebears.

This theme has not been lost on contemporary liturgical commentators. Aidan Kavanagh says that Christian worship has been transformed by a flight to Suburbia, his metaphor for the Church trying to escape the world, which he images as Civitas, the city. The liturgy should be the world's workshop, but the Church scorns the world in favor of attention to individual needs and desires. The old Civitas becomes a garbage dump for liturgical suburbanites:

**John F. Baldovin**, S.J.

> The workshop [of the Church in the world] relocates to suburbia
> and becomes no longer a civic affair but a series of cottage indus-
> tries producing novelties and fads for passing elites.[6]

Though Kavanagh's analysis is somber, even a little depressing,
and sounds like a liturgical commentary on George Orwell's *1984*
or Aldous Huxley's *Brave New World*, he makes a valid point. The
individualization of contemporary life, especially its affluence in
our own culture, makes not only for a Church out of touch with
justice but a Church out of touch with the world redeemed in
Christ, a Church that inevitably seeks a religious never-never land.

In a very different manner but with similar purpose, David
Power has called for a critical reappropriation of symbols—of liturgical life—by attending in a particular way to the memory of those
who are suffering, a memory we would most times like to avoid.[7]
These perceptive American liturgical commentators have made it
possible to begin evaluating the problem of incarnating a justice-
oriented understanding of the liturgical calendar from a new starting point. The starting point is all important, for if one begins by
presupposing that all that needs to be done is to add to the calendar and lectionary our immediate personal and social concerns,
then one has missed the point. The whole way in which we celebrate the liturgical year needs critical reflection. In order to understand the justice implications of the Christian calendar, one also
has to understand what it means and what it *has* meant to celebrate the year, at all, by means of a liturgical calendar.

## II. HOW HAS THE CALENDAR REFLECTED
## AND SHAPED CHRISTIAN BELIEF?

*Tension between the ''already—not-yet.''* Obviously how the calendar has reflected and shaped Christian belief is a question that
would take volumes to answer. We can only briefly develop three
points here. The first point is that the liturgical year always
manifests a real tension in the human and Christian experience of
time. The very fact of the incarnation of Christ and his redemption of the world implies an irreducible tension between the already and the not-yet in the Christian experience of the world.
We have been redeemed. God has definitively and irrevocably entered into the human condition and history; in a real sense, the
end—*telos*, goal—of the world has come. Yet at the same time, we

**Calendar for a Just Community**

must continue to work out our salvation. Creation, to employ Paul's metaphor in Romans 8:22, is still groaning in anticipation of its consummation. The world still struggles with pain, conflict, injustice, and other forms of sin. The experience of the death and resurrection of Christ, which is at the center of every liturgical celebration, means that Christians have faith in God's saving activity in the past and the present and at the same time are hopeful of that ultimate reconciliation and consummation mirrored in our Eucharistic praying and in the passage from Revelation quoted at the beginning of this essay. There is no better example of how this tension bears itself out in terms of the liturgical year than the annual celebration of Advent with its many-leveled appreciation of the coming of the Lord, an event that has been experienced and is yet to *be* experienced. The celebration of the liturgical year as an event of justice does not allow this tension to be resolved.

*Cultural Adaptation of the Calendar.* The second reflection is that liturgical communities have traditionally taken the skeletal structure of the existing local liturgical cycle, the main feasts and seasons, and used them as the framework for the celebration of Christianity within their own cultures. A good example of this is the connection between the Feast of the Unconquered Sun at Rome on December 25 in the late third and early fourth centuries and the Christian celebration of Christmas. Even if the origin of this dating of Christmas may lie elsewhere than the pagan solar feast, a theory that has recently been rehabilitated,[8] Christians did make use of the counter-symbolism of Christ the "Sun of Righteousness" for their own purposes. Such a cooptation of the pagan winter solstice and sun worship was not a betrayal of Christianity but rather the sensible adaptation of Christian faith to the existing culture. After all, if God has truly and irrevocably entered into the human condition and human history, then Christian faith can legitimately make use of the symbolism that the world provides. This insight is at the root of Christian sacramentality. To celebrate Christ, the light of the world, in the darkest days of the year—at least in the Northern hemisphere—makes a great deal of sense; it is not the survival of paganism but the recognition of God in nature and history.

Moreover, historical liturgical communities made their own social environment the setting for their worship. The cycle of the

**John F. Baldovin,** S.J.

year was spun out not only in terms of ideas and words, but in terms of places and events in the history of the people as well. This phenomenon is called stational liturgy, in which different churches and shrines served as the place of a city's main liturgical celebration depending on the feast or commemoration.[9] The best example of this liturgical-cultural phenomenon is the liturgical year in medieval Constantinople, the center—or better, the trend-setter—for much of late-Byzantine liturgy. Tenth-century sources show that the Church there held sixty-eight outdoor liturgical processions in the course of each year. These public manifestations of piety related Christian faith not only to events in the universal liturgical cycle like Easter and Christmas, but also to the saints and, in particular, to events in the history of the city itself. Many of the feasts were actually related to crucial moments in their social experience: the birthday or dedication of the city, a plague, an earthquake, the defeat of invaders in a siege. Here, God's power was made manifest and commemorated year after year in a tangible way to which people could relate; it was liturgy at its most popular.

*Importance of the Saints.* The theme of this conference is subtitled "An Owner's Guide." It seems appropriate to point out here that this is precisely what liturgy is at its best—owned by the people who celebrate it, relating their faith and worship to their experience of the world. This leads to the third point—the permanent attraction of saints' days in the Christian liturgical calendar. People relate best in the final analysis not to ideas but to flesh-and-blood human beings who exemplify for them in the contemporary cultural circumstances what it means to be *in Christ*, to be grasped by the power of God. Saints here are far more than models for moral imitation, they are tangible reminders that God's power has been at work in human beings. This is the reason behind the perennial fascination with shrines, relics, and images in Christian life—they are connectors with people who have manifested the truth and power of Christianity.[10] No doubt the popularity of various saints will wax and wane according to cultural and historical circumstances, but to abandon the saints for a rationalized Christomonistic approach to Christian faith is to impoverish not only the liturgical calendar but Christian faith itself. The caution here is that saints are never independent agents; they are always to be related to Christ, the Paschal Mystery, as is the source of their attractiveness. That devotion to the saints has at times in the history of Christianity been perverted does not negate its usefulness.

One need not look only to the medieval period to find examples of individuals who provide a powerful focus for the liturgical expression of Christian faith. In our own time, the Virgin of Guadalupe has served as an effective rallying point for a whole people's hopes for liberation and justice as well as an anchor for their Christian identity. A recent, fascinating study of devotion to the Virgin of Mount Carmel and her *festa* in Italian Harlem from the late nineteenth to the mid-twentieth century has shown how even in American culture such a devotion can be intimately involved in a people's self-realization and aspirations.[11]

These three factors: the tension between realized and expected redemption, the cultural adaptations of the liturgical calendar, and the importance of human examples have everything to do with discerning how the liturgical year can be a vehicle in the promotion of peace and justice.


### III. SOCIAL JUSTICE AND THE LITURGICAL YEAR TODAY

*Some Cautions.* The foregoing sections have been an attempt to show that we need to think about justice and the liturgical year at a popular level. How is the assembly's ownership of the liturgy ever to be experienced if we continue to work from abstract and elitist principles and not popular experience and needs? My fear is that most attempts to make the celebration of the liturgical year an authentic experience of and challenge to social justice will be perceived as the effort of an "enlightened" few to impose progressive political views on an unsuspecting—or perhaps increasingly suspicious—many. Such manipulation, to call it by its proper name, will never be effective in the long run, for it cannot appeal to the cultural experience of the people, nor can it help them to be counter-cultural in any confident fashion when the Gospel demands that they read the signs of the times in a discriminating manner. This is not to argue that liturgy and politics do not mix. Any manifestation of Christianity will be political in one way or another. However, it would be a perversion to make the liturgy a platform for a particular partisan political program. Such activity

**John F. Baldovin, s.j.**

106

destroys the liturgy's call to unity. On the other hand, to altogether avoid social issues—which always include politics—is irresponsible.

The second caution is that liturgy cannot do everything. It is unrealistic to imagine that an hour or so a week—and often less than that—of involvement in the liturgical assembly is going to be able to attune people to the value system and way of life to which the Gospel invites all Christians. The liturgy, supremely important as it is in the life of the Christian community, can only be the highpoint of Christian life set in the context of rich communal activity. To alert people to the need to do something about world hunger—in a homily or in other ways in the Sunday liturgy—and not to provide a means within parish life to actually work against hunger is superficial if not hypocritical; education about peace-and-justice issues from the pulpit can only be part of a wider parochial catechesis on the subject. The setting of the Sunday Eucharist does not allow significant time or dialogue for people to get involved in complex and sensitive issues like arms reduction, economic justice, racial and sexual discrimination, or the right to life, set in the context of the seamless-garment approach advocated these past years by Cardinal Bernardin and others. A parish with no active, extra-liturgical, adult-education-and-action committees is not likely to do much of substance in terms of addressing issues of justice.

How then can the liturgical year be an expression of the Christian vision of justice and peace celebrated in a community with an active commitment to these issues? (Needless to say there is a dialogical relation between the active commitment to justice issues and the impetus which the liturgy gives to working on them. In three areas, the celebration of the liturgical year can be improved as a calendar for a just community.

*A Sharper Focus: the Sunday Eucharist.* In the first place, social justice in the Eucharistic assembly's weekly practice is a prerequisite for the expression of social justice. The celebration of the Paschal Mystery every Sunday and the weekly rhythm that this celebration provides is the fundamental building block of the liturgical year. Robert Hovda has written that we don't need specially designated peace liturgies since every celebration of the Eucharist is, or *should* be, a peace liturgy.[12] To the extent that every liturgy manifests the same basic facts of our Christian existence, this is true. However, one needs to add that we do choose specific motifs, reflected by variable prayers and readings, to emphasize different aspects of Christian faith at different times; this is why we have a liturgical year in the first place. At the same time, what Hovda claims about peace and the liturgy is true of social justice as well. Each community needs to ask itself some hard questions about the weekly assembly in terms of the fundamental equality of the baptized as well as the potential activity of God in all human beings. Is there anyone excluded from the assembly on the basis of political, economic, or social status, gender, sexual preference, or race? Is there concern manifested, by the offerings of the assembly, for the poor and needy? Do the common prayers of the assembly always manifest in one way or another a concern for the needs of the world as well as the Church and individuals? Does the allocation of space and decoration reveal a community that has gathered as equals to praise and serve the Lord? Is the language employed in the liturgy inclusive?

One last question with regard to weekly practice is bound to bring us up short. Are the ministerial functions of the liturgy distributed in a manner that reflects charism, not status, gender, or race? Assigning ministerial functions to the non-ordained should be a relatively simple problem to solve. However, when it comes to the ordained, one encounters a certain frustration, for women and married men may not be ordained to the presbyterate and episcopacy in the Roman Catholic Church. Among other considerations, this is a justice issue. Until people can be ordained to ministry on the basis of their charisms, there will always be a certain injustice present in our liturgical assemblies.

The point here is that the whole of the liturgical year must reflect a concern with social justice and not simply certain special occasions. The formative work of the liturgy is gradual and subtle; it inculcates Christian identity by the pattern of worship repeated ritually week after week. This means that the way that the liturgy is celebrated every Sunday is going to have more of an impact on the assembly's orientation toward justice than special peak moments. In a sense, the liturgical year will be successful as an agent of justice when that aspect of Christian communal existence is taken for granted—not ignored—as one of the attitudes that describe the assembly's existence. If the Seventeenth Sunday of Or-

**John F. Baldovin, S.J.**

108

dinary Time reveals a justice orientation of the community, then special occasions that focus on social justice will be all the more effective. The clue is to look at the activity of the whole assembly and not merely at its ministers. To neglect reflection on the assembly's activity is to fall into the trap of regarding the liturgy as entertainment instead of primarily as the common action of God's people responding in the Holy Spirit.

A specific example may help to flesh this out. At Saint Francis de Sales Cathedral in Oakland, California, an assembly that includes a wide variety of Christian folk and has become fairly well-known throughout the United States, people do not sit down after they have received holy communion. They remain standing until everyone has received and the post-communion prayer has been said. Then all the people sit for a period of meditation that more often than not includes a choral piece. There is liturgical genius operative in this practice. If one wants to express the idea that communion means not only vertical union with the Lord but also horizontal union with one another by the sharing of the bread and the cup, then this belief is demonstrated most powerfully not only by words but also by actions. What better way than this relatively minor change in the assembly's physical disposition to imply that the Eucharist makes the communicants one, commits them to one another, and therefore acts as a mirror to reflect the successes, struggles, and failures in treating each other with reverence and love in daily life as well? As with all important areas of life, in liturgy, actions speak louder than words.

*The Lectionary.* In the second place, orientation toward justice in the liturgical year should be formed by the Church's lectionary. In the present theological climate, given the interest in the socio-cultural interpretation of Scripture as well as the leanings of liberation and political theologies, it should not be too difficult for preachers and those who prepare for liturgy to make use of these resources. Recent interpretation of the *Magnificat* (Luke 1:46-55) has concentrated on the socially subversive aspects of this Gospel canticle. The hungry are fed and the rich sent empty away; the mighty are cast down from their thrones and those of low degree have been exalted. Those who prepare liturgy should avoid spiritualizing a passage like this with its radical social implications. Strangely enough, this passage never serves as the gospel for a

Sunday, but it is employed on December 22 in preparation for Christmas, on May 31 for the Visitation, and on August 15 for the Assumption, as well as daily in Evening Prayer. It is possible to see in this passage a new kind of Marian piety, stressing God's preferential option for the poor. As we have already seen, such piety is an aspect of the celebration of the Virgin of Guadalupe.

Another example of the correct use of the lectionary for promoting a social-justice orientation to the liturgical year is an experience I had recently with the liturgical commission of the Diocese of Oakland. A group planning a Sunday liturgy focusing on AIDS-awareness had turned to the local Office of Worship for liturgical advice. Their response suggested choosing a Sunday on which the scriptural readings lent themselves readily to preaching on this theme. This was, of course, the correct instinct. Often one has the impression that themes are imposed on Sundays with no relation to the character of the Sunday liturgy itself. But there is no need to do this if liturgy planners are willing to accept the lectionary's lead in developing various motifs for different Sunday celebrations. Purists might object to this approach by claiming, correctly, that every Sunday is a celebration of the Paschal Mystery and that one of the major reforms of the current Roman Calendar is a restoration of Sunday to its pride of place in the liturgical year.[13] Formerly, the celebration of Sunday was easily superceded by saints' feasts and other commemorations. This much is true. However, calendars inevitably exhibit more growth than any other aspect of liturgy precisely because they have always responded to the concrete needs and piety of the people. Moreover, the fact that our weekly celebrations are variable with regard to the lectionary shows that the Paschal Mystery is always celebrated with one or another focus. As long as the lectionary is properly employed, it should be possible to recognize certain Sundays as particular occasions with special themes without abandoning the needed reform of the present calendar. It is the nature of calendars that such occasions come and go because cultures and needs change. One should expect that calendars need pruning from time to time. Therefore, designating certain Sundays in Ordinary Time for special observances should be a possibility even in the current calendar.

In addition to employing certain Sundays in Ordinary Time for the promotion of social justice, it is clear that the seasons of the

**John F. Baldovin, S.J.**

liturgical year provide valuable opportunities as well. Certainly the lectionary for Advent, as well as the eschatological thrust of the season itself, offers the challenge to envision the world anew, encouraged by the hope of God's ultimate reconciliatory power. Here, the figure of John the Baptist and the selections from the prophets—in particular, Isaiah—can speak powerfully to the need to attend to justice in our own time. The Easter season also provides an opportunity for a more socially sensitive celebration of the Good News with its weekly readings from the experience of the early community in the Acts of the Apostles, the record of the Church's outward mission to the world. Further, the second reading of this season in Cycle B is always taken from the Book of Revelation. No one reading contemporary commentaries on this biblical work can avoid the social implications of a community experiencing persecution and oppression.

One final comment needs to be made with regard to adapting social-justice themes to the lectionary. Music will be the key to effectively integrating these themes in communal worship. To employ lyrics and tunes that have a self-centered or sentimental effect—while emphasizing justice in the homily—is self-defeating. Here, as with the liturgical environment, the medium is the message. It is necessary for justice themes in the biblical readings and prayers to be matched with music that is mission oriented and expressive of a certain confidence in God's activity in the world as well as in individual lives.

*The Saints of the Calendar.* In the third place, the true promotion of justice in the liturgical year will result from attention to people, not causes. I have already asserted that a justice orientation to the liturgical year will not succeed if it is perceived as manipulation by an elite group imposing "radical" social, political, or economic ideas on the majority of the assembly. The best way to avoid this trap is to focus on individual examples of Christian lives that mirror a commitment to social justice. People relate to life stories in a way that they can never relate to abstract causes. This has always been the native genius of the calendar of the saints. I see this calendar as a resource for Christian worship rather than a series of commemorations consisting of variable prayers and an occasional special set of readings.[14] Certain saints like Martin de Porres, Peter Claver, and Francis and Clare of Assisi appeal readily to the

Christian social conscience. In addition, it seems opportune to commemorate unofficial contemporary saints, a few of whom I mention with their memorial days: Dorothy Day (November 29), Martin Luther King, Jr. (the third Monday of January), the Four Women Martyrs of El Salvador (Maura Clark, Jean Donovan, Ita Ford, and Dorothy Kazel, December 2), Archbishop Oscar Romero (March 24), Dietrich Bonhoeffer (April 9), Rutilio Grande (March 12), and Dag Hammarskjold (September 18). Certain liturgical communities may want to celebrate these unofficial contemporary saints on their anniversaries, but an incorporation of these figures into the preaching and prayers of the Sunday assembly, especially if aspects of their lives and deaths can throw light on the lectionary readings, would be more likely. The greatest and most powerful source for Christian reflection on peace and justice in the liturgical year is Jesus of Nazareth. However, one should bear in mind that Christians have traditionally turned to holy individuals—those reflecting the truth of the Gospel in Jesus—with whom they could relate culturally as well.

*Ember Days.* A final note on specific occasions for the promotion of justice in the liturgical calendar concerns Ember Days, one aspect of the traditional Roman calendar whose observance has been left to the discretion of national conferences of bishops.[15] These celebrations on Wednesdays, Fridays, and Saturdays in the spring, summer, fall, and winter of each year originally had a penitential—or better, supplicatory—flavor, asking God for favorable weather. Such celebrations obviously need to be remodeled in a post-agrarian society. Perhaps civic occasions that have also become relatively popular as liturgical observances in the American Church already meet this need. Certainly Thanksgiving, Labor, Memorial, and Independence Days are well suited to this effort to relate individual liturgical assemblies to wider social needs in the context of imploring God's aid.[16] The Sacramentary already contains special prayers and prefaces for Thanksgiving and for July 4. In addition, votive Masses such as the ones provided for peace and for a blessing on human labor can be used creatively for such combined civic and religious celebrations. Much more can be done, it seems to me, to relate the penitential focus of Lent to social needs, though to be sure it is not its only aspect. Fasting and asceticism can well be directed to consciousness of hunger and poverty as any number of movements have recently demonstrated.

**John F. Baldovin, s.j.**

CONCLUSION

The many justice issues and concerns that face our contemporary world—the arms race, poverty, homelessness, famine, racism, discrimination because of gender or sexual preference, oppression in Latin America or Eastern Europe, health care, the rights of the disabled and the elderly, respect for life—can all be integrated into the liturgical year. But they must be integrated in a way that meets with popular acceptance and that respects the nature of the liturgical calendar itself. A religious faith is worthless if it has nothing to offer the needs that people experience. Those needs are reflected in the Scriptures that we read week after week in the rich Christian tradition. Although the challenge to justice in an affluent and self-centered society is great, great also is our confidence in the Spirit that empowers Christians. The struggle for justice and peace is not ours alone.

NOTES

1. National Conference of Catholic Bishops, "Economic Justice for All," par. 56 (Washington: United States Catholic Conference, 1986).

2. *Ibid.* par. 325.

3. James A. Sanders, "Canon and Calendar: An Alternative Lectionary Proposal," in D. Hessel, ed., *Social Themes of the Christian Year* (Philadelphia: Westminster Press, 1983) 258.

4. Richard Sennett, *The Fall of Public Man* (New York: Alfred A. Knopf, 1977).

5. Robert Bellah et al., *Habits of the Heart: Individualism and Commitment in American Life* (Berkeley: University of California Press, Ltd., 1985) 219–49.

6. Aidan Kavanagh, *On Liturgical Theology* (New York: Pueblo Publishing Co., 1984) 45.

7. David N. Power, *Unsearchable Riches* (New York: Pueblo Publishing Co., 1984) see pp. 172–210.

8. Thomas J. Talley, *The Origins of the Liturgical Year* (New York: Pueblo Publishing Co., 1986) 87–99.

9. John F. Baldovin, "The City as Church, the Church as City," *Liturgy* 3:4 (1983) 69–73.

10. See Peter Brown, *The Cult of the Saints* (Chicago: University of Chicago Press, 1981).

**Calendar for a Just Community**

11. See Robert A. Orsi, *The Madonna of 115th Street* (New Haven: Yale University Press, 1986).

12. Robert Hovda, "The Amen Corner," *Worship* 57 (1983) 438–43.

13. *General Norms for the Liturgical Year and Calendar*, par. 4, Liturgy Documentary Series 6, United States Catholic Conference (Washington: United States Catholic Conference, 1984), 14.

14. John F. Baldovin, "On Feasting the Saints," *Worship* 55 (1980) 342–44.

15. *General Norms for the Liturgical Year*, pars. 45–47.

16. See Richard Eslinger, "Civil Religion and the Year of Grace," *Worship* 58 (1984) 372–83.

Gertrud Mueller Nelson

# Christian Formation of Children: The Role of Ritual and Celebration

"PRECESSION"

Some years ago, I spent an afternoon caught up in a piece of sewing I was doing. The waste basket near my sewing machine was filled with scraps of fabric cut away from my project. This basket of discards was a fascination to my daughter, Annika, who, at the time, was still three years old. She rooted through the scraps searching out the long bright strips of cloth, collected them to herself, and went off. When it had been silent too long, I took a moment to check on her and tracked her whereabouts to the back garden. I found her there, sitting in the grass with a long pole she had gotten from the garage. She was fixing the scraps to the top of the pole with great sticky wads of tape. Mothers sometimes ask foolish questions, and I asked one. I asked her what she was doing. Without taking her eyes from her work she said, "I'm making a banner for a precession [sic]. I need a precession so that God will come down and dance with us." With that, she solemnly lifted her banner to flutter in the wind, and slowly she got up to dance.

I don't think that Annika was a particularly precocious toddler. I think, rather, she was doing what three year olds do when left to

**Gertrud Mueller Nelson**

their natural and intuitive religious sense, and I was simply fortunate to hear and see what she was about. Mothers often hear wonderful things from their youngsters. We are the anthropologists, if you will, and our children are the exotic primitives who also happen to be under foot. This small primitive allowed me to witness a holy moment, and I learned all over again how strong and real is that sense of wonder that children have—how innate and easy their way with the sacred. She had all the necessary elements for a religious ritual: a thing and an action. Here, religion was child's play. I had to wonder what happens in our development that as adults we become a serious folk, uneasy in our relationship with God, out of touch with the mysteries we knew in childhood, restless, empty, searching to regain a sense of awe and a way, once again, to "dance with God."

Indeed, I had to wonder what happens to our children on their way to adulthood that they become *too quickly* alienated from their religious sense and become the small monsters that even a Thomas Merton had observed. The modern child, he noted, may early in his or her existence have natural inclinations toward spirituality. The child "may have imagination, originality, a simple and individual freshness of response to reality and even a tendency to moments of thoughtful silence and absorption." All these tendencies, however, are soon destroyed by the dominant culture. The child "becomes a yelling, brash, false little monster, brandishing a toy gun and dressed up like some character he has seen on television. His head is filled with inane slogans, songs, noises, explosions, statistics, brand names, menaces, ribaldries and cliches." Then, when the child goes to school, he learns "to verbalize, to rationalize, to pose, to make faces like an advertisement, to need a car and in short, to go through life with an empty head, conforming to others like himself, in 'togetherness'" (From *The Inner Experience*, St. Joseph's Abbey, Spencer, MA 01562).

I think we can say that our "fall from innocence" is a fact of the human condition. But I think that as parents and teachers, we have to consider our own role in *shoving* children out of the garden of their original innocence too soon, too harshly, without any tools for understanding the frantic actions that send each one in hungry search for an unknown and unnamed entity. For it is also a fact of the human condition that, once banished from the garden, *we never stop longing and seeking to be made whole again.*

**Christian Formation of Children**

Life's tasks of learning to think and compare, to sort and choose began with our first taste of "knowledge of good and evil," and for that fruit we have developed a great appetite. It is, in fact, knowledge that changes our innocent relationship with God. And we spend the rest of our days circling the garden of our original innocence, yearning to find our way back in.

Unless we become again as little children—but as little children who know their own hearts—we cannot enter the kingdom of heaven. Our way back to a connection with God is through the profound experience of our humanity. When we live artfully the mysteries of our humanness, we will know our hearts; we will see beyond the obvious to the mysteries hidden in the ordinary. For the route we choose to the kingdom is marked with the mysteries of the human condition: births and deaths, joys and sufferings, peak experiences and pitfalls. And when we are struck with the *meaning* of our most human experiences, we are most closely connected with the divine.

So then, it is in the mysteries of our humanity—of our human developmental cycles—of our everyday feelings, our pains, failures and triumphs, meetings and partings, birthing, living, dying and rising again where we may suddenly recognize God, and these are the occasions which we encircle, compelled to *do* something in celebration and recognition and invitation to the transcendent.

The Church in her poetic aspect—which has always been there for us and has always been centered in the cycles of our human development—nourishes us through rite and symbol, through rhythmic repetition, through liturgical action. The poetic Church celebrates our cycles and seasons, inviting us to be fully human, asking us to see and engage and feel and touch and taste and be aware and grow and be transformed. Through our celebration of the Church cycle, through custom and liturgy, through sacrament and sacramental, through rituals and holy folklore and holy play, the personal experiences which make up our daily lives are affirmed and made sacred.

Furthermore, this creative and poetic Church helps us to pay full attention to what the dominant culture would have us deem ordinary and commonplace. Rituals and symbols use the ordinary things in life. We have to remind ourselves daily to preserve for our children the holiness of everyday things. We have to develop

**Gertrud Mueller Nelson**

an art of living, a sacramental mentality, for the transcendent is disclosed in what is wonderfully simple and familiar—indeed, in bread, wine, fire, ash, earth, water, oil, tears, seeds, songs, feastings and fastings, pains and joys, bodies and thoughts, regressions and transformations. Christian ritual draws its action from what is most human in us more than from heady ideas from theology. Liturgy is not an idea; it is not knowledge dressed up in gestures. It is simply up and *doing* in bodily action what the heart already knows.

It is the role of the creative teacher and the thoughtful parent to nurture the natural religious sense of their children and their own inner, forgotten child, I might add. We must protect them as long as we can from the clamor of the world and what it tells them they need to buy for their fulfillment. We must help them to know their own soul and provide or perfect the rituals and forms that will touch the places of life's mysteries and give them back meaning—not a sentimentalized meaning but a meaning that they will never outgrow.

A return to the creative function of the Church, its myth, rites, and symbols, is a step forward in this nurturance. It builds on our natural sense of what is holy and returns us to the sacred when we have become flooded and numbed with the clamors of the world. Rites and celebrations provide the ultimate religion lesson: *a recognition that God is revealed in our humanness.*

SO WHEN WAS THE LAST TIME
THAT GOD REVEALED HIMSELF TO YOU?

I live near the beach, and often I watch how children respond to the ocean. I watched, once, how three children stood with considerable awe before the grand ocean as it rose up in huge waves and repeatedly crashed onto the beach. The powerful water was not to be rushed into lightly or with abandon. They regarded the whole drama in silence as they clung to their mother's legs. Then with a little daring, the oldest launched an age-old ritual which we can all remember having performed ourselves and which we can see repeated over and over again wherever there are small children at the beach. The child turned her back on what was too awesome, and she began to dig a hole. Her brothers joined her. They dug and scooped the sand until they had a sizeable hollow, and slowly they allowed something of the great sea to enter and

**Christian Formation of Children**

fill their hole. It became their mini-sea. It was a body of water that they could easily encompass and control. In time, they stomped in the puddle and splashed with abandon in a way that they were not yet willing to do in the surf. Then the surf rose higher and swished into their hole, wiping out one of its walls. With a delicious mixture of thrill and horror, they repeatedly rebuilt their walls, and the ocean repeatedly washed them down. Their manageable sea always let in something of the unmanageable. This was a game that they were able to play for a very long time. For them, it was a religious experience. They had created a hole to catch something of the transcendent.

For us, this story is the paradigm for ritual making. Ritual and ceremony are the container we create to hold something of a mystery. We all seek the container that can carry the touch of God for us. It is natural to us as human beings to make rituals because we are, by nature, religious people.

### THE SYMPTOMATIC WAY

Even in this very secular world that no longer centers itself in the religious, our quest for "something more" cannot be denied. Today, we are not likely to take our children on pilgrimage to visit holy shrines with the bones of saints or the tunic of Mary. *But we all still go on pilgrimage*—we still have our meccas. Disneyland may be such a "holy land" where God is rendered Mickey Mouse. Our religious nature is still at the root of who we have become. We may think that over time we have shrugged off all manner of "empty" religious rituals and ceremonies, but it turns out that we have only created a vacuum, a void which is quickly filled either by offerings from the secular world which knows our hunger and can profit from it or by unconscious rituals we put in place of the ancient rituals whose meaning has faded.

We are not as free to choose or not choose our rituals and symbolic behavior as we may think. Actually, our only choice is between conscious rituals and unconscious ones—those which enrich, dignify, and enliven our lives and interactions and those which enslave us, which deaden life and block us from deep human relationship and meaning.

Without a way to consciously feed and express our basic religious nature, we allow our religious experiences to enter through the back door in the manner of our habits, our fears, our neuroses

**Gertrud Mueller Nelson**

and symptoms. In place of the periodic, holy fast, for instance, we have become slaves to our perennial diets. In exchange for "carrying our cross" in the constructive suffering that every life requires, we complain of low-back pain. The old taboos from which we think we are freed crop up as new varieties of superstitions for which we take another vitamin. The neurotic is religious material done unconsciously. Neurosis is the modern parody of religion and is the consequence of our lost orientation to the sacred.

When we recognize the holy nature of the moment and understand the meaning of a given experience, we can make it holy with a ritual. If we don't honor that moment with a conscious ritual, an unconscious solution will come forward to deal with what we are trying to face.

### GOING TO BED

Let me give you an example—putting a small child to bed. Mother is in the kitchen mashing avacado for a dip and watching the oven so that the meringue on the top of her pie doesn't burn. Guests are about to arrive, and she is caught up in making her preparations for dinner. Dad is on a ladder outside the front door replacing a light bulb. Small Teddy has been sent off to bed with shouted reminders to brush his teeth, not eat the toothpaste, and wash behind his ears. Then Mother rushes in for a quick hug, tucks him in, and turns out the light.

Any one of us observing this scene knows already that this isn't going to work. Bedtime is a very big transition for a small child to make. Transitions are fraught with uncertainty and danger. It is difficult to give oneself over to the darkness when the primordial fear of being abandoned or left to wild beasts is still an inner reality. But Mother hurries down the hall to her lemon meringue pie, and, of course, she hears the patter of little feet right behind her. "But I want to see if the company has come, but I only want to kiss you, but I don't like it all dark." So Mother hustles Teddy back into bed, not once, but several times while Teddy with an ingenuity that astounds, whips up a bedtime ritual for himself that he hopes will bring him a little security. This ritual includes another hug for Daddy, the light put on in the bathroom, a night light installed in his room. He badly wants a bedtime story, and if Mother's not game, he'd be glad to tell a long-winded one himself. He needs half a zoo of stuffed animals tucked into bed with

**Christian Formation of Children**

him along with three of his favorite trucks. Mother finally flies to her meringue pie which she discovers smoking and black in the oven. And from the hall, we hear Teddy: "I need a drink!"

From this common experience, we can see why most of the religious rituals that we know are centered around times of transition. Teddy's parents would have far greater success with their son if they would first understand that Teddy is not being a bad boy. He is afraid. His hard-won daylight consciousness is difficult to give up to the darkness without some protection and comfort. Teddy, because he is still a child, doesn't have the skills to devise a *conscious ritual* for himself, but he *is* devising a ritual—an unconscious one—to deal with the mysteries of the dark. Wise parents will have created a comforting routine for putting this little boy to bed, the child having provided some of the ingredients for this ritual. It will be a ritual that is both practical—we get bathed and brushed—and reassuring. This ritual will be basically the same every night. It may include a retelling of the events of the day, a story, and certainly night prayers. A blessing, perhaps with the Easter water brought home from the Vigil service, will guard against fear and give strength. A kiss, a firm and certain "good night," and Teddy knows that now it is safe to go to sleep.

### ADULT BEDTIME

Without conscious rites to close the day, even the enlightened adult can come up against some curious compulsions, habits, or superstitious behaviors which are an attempt to close the day and guard against the powerful and unknown elements of the unconscious. Imagine the adult who goes to bed. Have you ever settled into bed and then wondered if you locked the back door? You get up to check again. While you're up anyway, maybe you'll fix yourself a little cup of something hot to help you sleep. You make another trip to the bathroom, check in the mirror again—those crows feet around the eyes need a dab of cream. You crawl into bed—blast! Did you turn the gas off after you heated your milk? Better check. You pad down the hall again. It was off, but you can never be too sure. Now, back to bed. You slip in. You pull up the covers. You settle down. Ah! But you forgot to close the closet door! Unclear about what the fear is and distracted from a more meaningful way to close the day, you are driven through your routines until you finally sleep.

**Gertrud Mueller Nelson**

No wonder that the Benedictine Rule offered clear, consistent, comforting, disciplined ways to deal with bedtime—in fact, with every transition of the day.

The most important ceremonies in our human cycles have to do with transitions, helping us to get from one level to the next. During transitions, we are vulnerable and in danger. Like the creature who has outgrown an old skin and can wear it no longer, we shed what is no longer fitting. But thus exposed, we are in a state of crisis; we feel soft and unprotected and unsure of the future "skin" that is still unknown to us. In times of transition, we are tempted to turn back to our old ways: these are at least warm and familiar to us; the new is frightening and unfamiliar. But we know how unsuccessful are our attempts at crawling back into an old and worn-out skin.

Colin Turnbull, in his marvelous accounting of the Mbuti peoples of Zaire, passes along to us their understanding of the dangers in transition. (From *The Human Cycle,* Simon and Schuster, 1983.) The Mbuti see the person as being in the center of a sphere. In moving from here to there, the sphere moves too and offers protection. If movement in time or space is too sudden or vehement, we risk the danger of reaching the boundaries of the sphere too quickly, before the center has time to catch up. When this happens, persons become *wazi-wazi* or disoriented and unpredictable. If they pierce through the safe boundaries of the sphere into the other world, they risk letting in something else which takes their place. If the Mbuti know of and guard against such violent and sudden motion—and that without the experience of automobiles or jet planes—what do we, the so-called civilized people of the world, know of our transitions in space and time? I think we are a whole society in a state of *wazi-wazi,* beside ourselves, possessed by imposter selves.

Even though most of our everyday transitions may be small ones—going to bed or getting up in the morning, driving to work or coming home at night—we know them to be powerful the minute we recognize the agitation and the pent up feelings that we carry at those moments. Transitions are by their very nature difficult and psychologically and spiritually dangerous because we are tempted to regress. That is the reason I don't like to talk to anyone in the morning until I have had my first cup of coffee. That is why my shoulders ache while I fight my way through the traffic

**Christian Formation of Children**

as I drive home at night. That is why I find it so difficult to deal with the pile of mail that waits for me inside the door as I step into the house. My own children have pointed out to me that when I return home after an extended trip away, I head straight for the kitchen which I seem to hold as my personal territory and begin to wipe counters and sweep the floor. Irritated because the kitchen has actually been *used* by others during my absence, the imposter mother has arrived and bustles around giving orders. And my children comment: "Mother's riding her broom again."

Of course, there are transitions to be dealt with on a grand scale too: birthing and dying are the ultimate transitions, and rebirth and our final resurrection are actually what all this small stuff is about. We are practicing at our ultimate transitions and final transformation by muddling through the "terrible twos" of our own unsung, mid-life crisis.

It is appropriate to pay attention to the feelings that we go through at the great moments of transition in our lives. These are opportunities to point up, with consciousness, the change, the transformation, that we are invited to make. Here, through ritual or ceremony, we find courage and communal or individual support. A ritual or a celebration of the moment will invite a feeling discharge and offer safety to the person at risk. While we shed our old ways and embrace a new way, a ceremony will make the sacred experience taste both bitter and sweet. We rejoice at weddings because we are witness to a new and profound beginning, but we might also cry, because we are witness to the end of an era. The first day of school may be exciting and hold great promise. The first day of school may also fill one with fear and feelings of loss. I know a school that has the most delightful celebrations for Valentine's Day. But in their wisdom it is not all lace and ice cream. The children have special presentations and discussions about their own friendships—about social cliques, about gossip, about feelings of rejection or inferiority. Rites are meant to engage both halves of the truth, the dark and the light, because a half truth is sentimentality or a lie. Good ceremony continually deals with both sides of a question in order to arrive at a place that can contain them both.

In the classroom, in the parish, it is the creative teacher and planner who knows that we need forms and rituals and ceremonies within which to express ourselves and be nourished and safe.

**Gertrud Mueller Nelson**

The *art* of making this form a form which nourishes is far more important than the other administrative services that often bog us down. Ritual making and ceremony require leaders who are not afraid to recognize their talent or insight and are willing to step forward to use it. Before we can plan the larger liturgies, we must be sensitive to the minor cycles, the daily moments that need recognition, consciousness, and an artful ritual.

When I taught at an East-coast school in the days of its founding, it was easy to recognize that our administrators were so caught in the throes of administration and the constantly changing aspects of a new school—in daily re-inventions of the wheel—that I offered to create a service which we then called "All-School Celebrations." The celebrations were meant to make some things in our lives certain and unchanging. They centered around the issues of transition and high feeling—anger, fear, excitement, disappointment, success, envy, joy. In time, these celebrations or simple rituals covered everything from how we greeted the children at the door each morning or dismissed them in the afternoon, to how the whole school prayed and sang together each morning. They affected how the teachers ate together in the lounge, how we relieved tensions or helped the children to get rid of extra energy or fear: rituals that engage feelings fully and then discharge them. They covered the basketball games between the children and the staff, how we prepared the children and brought them to Mass, how we celebrated Advent as a whole school or prepared a class for first Eucharist, how we dealt with the deaths of some members in our community, or how we greeted the birth of a student's new sibling.

We carefully studied our attraction to the power of symbol— from birthday cakes to school awards and diplomas. We included many symbols of transformation. We made jam and churned butter. We planted gardens and tended a compost pile. We learned that we could make an art of any of life's tasks from washing the chalk boards to mending the stone fences. We aligned our school year with the Church year and drew from her sacraments and sacramentals. We looked to anthropology and folklore for further richness and ideas for dealing with the human events of a school community in formation. It was gratifying to visit that school twenty years later and find some things still firmly entrenched as part of the character and identity of that school. If you are a

**Christian Formation of Children**

teacher and have devised something that is powerfully satisfying, keep it and perfect it and spread it around the school. For "school spirit" is not to be found or formed only on the playing field. School spirit is God's Spirit as expressed in our creative approach to human history, human situations.

### HOME RITUALS

In the same way, in a family, parents need to provide a structure and form that safeguards and feeds all of its members. There are the daily cycles to pay attention to, the yearly cycles, and there is the human cycle, common to all of us. A birthday celebration, beyond the birthday candles, can engage the whole family in this moment of personal history. The birthday child loves to hear the story of how she was born—every wonderful detail. She wants to hear, every year, how it was thirty below zero that night and Papa had to push the car to get it started. She wants to know about the baby clothes her mother packed in her bags before her trip to the hospital. The family looks at the old baby books, and the birthday child sits at the head of the table while all present take a turn to say what is special about her and what they like so much about her. The birthday child has a chance to talk about the great events of the past year and her hopes and fears for the year ahead.

In our house, birthday children, to help them engage this day as a developmental step, are given two envelopes. One is marked "Privilege": "Now that you are eight years old you may ride your bicycle as far as Maple Street!" The other envelope is marked "Responsibility": "Now that you are eight years old, you must help the household by scrubbing the bathroom sinks every Saturday morning before you go off to play." The beauty of that one is that the distinction between "privilege" and "responsibility" wasn't made in the early years. I remember a wail coming out of the bathroom from my daughter Sara when she was about eight. "Someone already cleaned the sink and it was my *privilege!*" At sixteen, the envelope may hold a key to the family car, and the responsibility covers the task of a periodic oil change. Such a ceremony allows the child to see life as process and developmental stages.

In families, we need to reevaluate the rituals we already have and discern if they are worthy and conscious of whatever mystery

**Gertrud Mueller Nelson**

we are trying to engage. Mealtime in the American family is in a state of disrepair. How ever can we understand the Eucharist if the family meal does not allow us to "know Him in the breaking of the bread?" We need to devise ways of marking important moments—little moments and grand ones. We need some private rites of passage for our children—not as powerful, perhaps, as communal, tribal rites of other cultures but better than the school proms and drinking parties that our culture offers. We need ways to leave home in our youth and ways to enter retirement as we grow old. We need ways to prepare for new life and ways to face our own death. At its core, a rite or ceremony points us, through our human experiences, to the transcendent. Through rites, we raise what is happening to us to a level of conscious awareness, and in doing so we actively seek to be transformed.

### THE CYCLE OF THE CHURCH YEAR

Since we've considered our daily, human experiences, it may not come as a surprise that the feasts and seasons of the Church year correspond closely to and are the grace-filled, practice fields of our personal cycles. Advent celebrates the marriage of heaven to earth and our anticipation of the birth of the God-man. It connects us to every sort of waiting and pregnancy that our personal lives might ever know, from waiting for the bus to healing the split between what is every day and earthly and the inspiration of spirit. Christmas brings us a Saviour and new hope. The mystery of the Incarnation makes all matter holy because God found the human body, the barnyard, and the company of peasants the perfect setting for his Son. Lent offers us the opportunity to suffer and to die to our false selves. Through the Lord's own passion, we learn to understand the sufferings that weave in and out of our daily lives—the necessary crosses that are prerequisite to the glorious transformation of the Easter mysteries.

From the feasts and mysteries of the Church year, we draw the sort of nourishment that is the only antidote I know to the false, poisoning versions of life and meaning concocted and served up by our consumer culture. By celebrating through the structure of the Church, we actually are given the forms we need to become whole, and we are given the formulas to make whole every human experience. This effort requires our rediscovery of the themes which the cycle of the Church calendar offers us and the

**Christian Formation of Children**

application of our creative imagination to the rites and folk customs already available. Then, through the celebration of the sacred
mysteries, we will find new meaning in the inexplicable and a
worthy container for what we realize in our hearts. That means
that in the parish community, in the school, and in the family, if
we are honest about living the themes of the Church calendar, we
must come to know and touch and be touched by the mysteries of
that season.

### ADVENT

Using Advent as a case in point, we immerse ourselves in the
spirit of the season—together with our immediate community and
with all the ages of people who have gone before us and will
come after us—to *wait* and fully engage what it means to be
spiritually pregnant. Waiting is something we all hate to do. We
hate it so much that we have invented instant coffee, plastic grass,
Concorde airplanes, and "hold music" for the telephone.

But waiting is something we already know as a reality in our
lives. Much as we are tempted to fight against it, we know it to
be a valuable fact of life. To pull the cake out of the oven too
soon, simply because we can't wait any longer, only gives us a
runny cake. Waiting is necessary, the vital ingredient to anything
of quality or value: a ripened fruit, a healthy baby, a work of art,
a reconciled relationship. It is also necessary to a healthy Christmas. Because we hate to wait, the commercial world urges us to
jump the gun, and by the time Christmas actually comes we are
sick of it all—the tree is dry, Santa Claus is old hat, and the new
blouse is the wrong size. Somehow, the arrival of the new life has
been aborted, and there is no healthy satisfying Christmas.

For this reason, I think it is the job of the parish and school
community and caring parents to learn again the *art of waiting* and
then to teach it. Waiting is not some punishment that the Church
imposes on us, but rather it is the discipline that enhances our ap- ·
preciation of life and makes it healthy. Advent invites us to un-
derscore and understand with a new patience that very feminine
state of being, waiting. Our masculine world wants to blast it
away, and we see as progressive every device invented that
eliminates what we have learned to see as time wasted. But
studies show that that time saved is not necessarily time given
back to us to live more humanly. We tend rather only to speed up

**Gertrud Mueller Nelson**

our action and our busy-ness. Waiting is unpractical time, good for nothing, but mysteriously necessary for all that is becoming. Brewing, baking, simmering, fermenting, ripening, germinating, gestating are the feminine processes of becoming, and they are the symbolic states of being which belong in a life of value, *necessary to transformation*. Ultimately, the deep-seated chauvinism of our culture which despises this feminine element in life is well illustrated in our general inability to celebrate the season of Advent.

It is always surprising to me how many Church schools and parishes—communities which should be the examples and inspiration to us all—offer Christmas programs during this sacred time of waiting. To use the excuse that we don't have the children over Christmas is to misunderstand our mission to teach the spirit of the liturgy. Advent as a time for preparation and anticipation is also a time filled with liturgical encouragement, folk customs, and Advent songs and carols. But none of these exercises in waiting make any sense if they are overlaid with Christmas decorations and parties. Even our efforts at gathering the greens and weaving our Advent wreath as symbol of our waiting and preparation is thus relegated to a meaningless gimmick or cute decoration.

ADVENT WREATH AS SYMBOL

The Advent wreath, on the other hand, as a serious "outward sign" has a powerful symbolic function. For the power of symbol puts us directly in touch with a force or an idea by use of an image or an object. A "thing" can do that for us. But for that to happen, we have to get involved in it, in its making and using, in its fragrance and its light. Most of all, we have to remember that the Advent wreath was once a wagon wheel—a wheel *removed* and rendered *useless* and inactive. It is the sacrifice of an everyday object, taken for granted and ever rotating, now stopped and brought indoors as a sign of a different time, *sacred time*, a time to halt action and turn inward. The recovery of hope, in the year's darkest season, can only be accomplished when we have had the courage to stop and wait and engage fully in the winter of our dark longing. Then the symbolic reality of an Advent wreath has deep and penetrating power. It bridges the gulf between knowing and believing. It integrates mind and heart.

It is also important to remember that at the core of the major rituals that we choose or create for home and parish, it is wise to

**Christian Formation of Children**

keep a character which is broader and richer and deeper than a too-narrow personal piety or a disjointed array of spontaneous actions and reactions. We use forms that carry to some extent a symbolic essence and that are rooted in the past, yet are a living expression that have helped many people to know themselves and express themselves. A broad approach in the actions and words and objects we choose will, like good liturgy, transcend the private, the immediate, and connect us with the rest of humankind, giving a sense of unity and purpose that will not leave us caught in our own narrow world.

This broader approach is also important in creating family rituals. It is the difference between putting out marshmallows on the windowsill for Santa's elves rather than putting straws into the manger during Advent for good deeds done in preparation for the coming of the Child. When children grow up and express their spiritual independence and reject the narrow familial realm, they will, if parents have grounded them in Scriptural language and a deep, spiritual heritage, find that meaning to be still available to them, and certain customs will continue to nourish and hold meaning for them. Sentimentality, poor taste, ugly forms, trite expressions, artificial greens, and fake snow do not hold over time. Rather, the oldest customs and traditions often hold the kind of richness which we need never outgrow. For this reason, we have to keep looking at and talking over the visual shape we give to the sacred world and its hidden events.

CHRISTMASTIDE

Of course it is important to remember—with all the longing, the excitement, the counting of days, the anticipation, and happy preparations that we engage in while we await the coming of the Saviour—that we don't go through all that to celebrate for a single day. We celebrate all twelve days of Christmas, and there are folk customs for almost every one of those days that follow Christmas. In our parish, we end the season with a party on the Feast of Epiphany. It seems wonderfully appropriate for a school to welcome the children back from their long Christmas vacation with a grand closure of the season still to look forward to.

Some of the high points of our own parish celebration may serve as examples of how to celebrate Epiphany either on a small scale with the family or on a large scale with a parish community

**Gertrud Mueller Nelson**

or school. The whole parish arrives, young and old, on the night before Epiphany or on the evening of Epiphany itself. We sing all the Christmas carols we know for the last time that season. We have three large cakes, one for the small children, one for the teenagers, and one for the adults. In each cake, a navy bean is hidden. Those who find the beans become the kings, Casper, Melchior, and Balthazar, and are the royal representatives of their age groups. They are robed and crowned on the spot and cheered by their loyal subjects. Then accompanied by kazoos and horns, coffee-can drums and rattling car keys, the whole company of loyal subjects sings "We Three Kings" and follows their kings in procession into the gym—in our case, the church, because we have no other large space. A large star at the top of a pole is at the head of the procession and halts at a given place. Now the kings must embark on a wild Parcheesi game where the points of a star are spun and fate dictates the number of steps that they may take on their arduous journey toward Bethlehem—the creche at the altar. In our parish, we arrange a "living Bethlehem" and give a role to all the smaller children who are now dressed as Mary and Joseph, shepherds, and angels and are arranged and waiting at the foot of the altar.

The kings, waiting at the back of the church, move from one "stepping stone" to the next, and when they have used up their number of steps, they read the verdict under their feet. "You have forgotten to water your camels—go back to the oasis." "You have lost sight of the star; go back to square one." "Friendly shepherds point the way; go forward three steps." "Sandstorms are forecast; hole up for one turn." Field and fountain, moor and mountain, and finally they come to Herod's castle. They have a serious encounter with Herod who awaits them there. Herod is played by an adult who, in his own oily way, questions the kings to find out their motives for wanting to find the Child and asks them to return to him with information and directions. The whole assembly hisses at that one. But otherwise, cheering and clapping, each age group urges on their own king.

Last time, when things got very tense and close, it was marvelous to see St. Joseph, up front, drop his staff and start pounding his knees and shout, "Come on Balthazar! You can make it!" when it looked like his king was going to win. When all the kings finally arrive and the Bethlehem scene has settled down again into

**Christian Formation of Children**

position, we hear the Gospel story of the Magi read to us once more, an echo of the Epiphany liturgy. Our pastor gives a little homily. Then every family is sent home with a piece of blessed chalk to mark the doorways of their homes in a special and old ceremony for the blessing of homes on Epiphany. It is a delightful way to act out the Gospel and to consider the journey on which we all find ourselves as we take two steps forward and one step back in our daily search for the Christ.

This communal celebration of the feast of Three Kings is just one example of how a community can end its Christmas celebrations with a true climax and head into the new year refreshed and sustained. It seems to be the perfect antidote to any possible after-Christmas blues. Variations of this celebration, if they cannot be carried off by the parish, are the perfect occasion for family and neighborhood celebrations. It seems to be the perfect antidote to any possible after-Christmas blues. Variations of this celebration, if they cannot be carried off by your parish, are the perfect occasion for family and neighborhood celebrations. The last of the fruit-cakes and cookies are served. A king or kings are elected with the fate of the bean-cake. The lintel over the door is blessed with the markings of the Three Kings and the date of the new year: 19 C + M + B + 90. And finally, the tree is taken down in ceremony and with reverent finality.

There are celebrations to follow in the coming months—one last fling at Mardi Gras precedes our Lenten feast. There are endless helps that encourage us to engage our fast and to be reconciled to one another. These cannot all be mentioned here, but there are many detailed examples in my book *To Dance with God*. It is right to remember that the liturgies of the Church year are enhanced and pointed up by our communal efforts. And community is enhanced and strengthened by our joint feasts and fasts.

While there are many, many more occasions to consider for celebrations during the Church year—unfortunately, we have not the space here—it seems right that we consider briefly the issue of our Easter celebrations.

### A COPTIC EASTER

A few years ago, a film on public television showed the Easter vigil services as they were celebrated in a Coptic church in Jerusalem. In the dead of night, hundreds of people gathered in the Ca-

**Gertrud Mueller Nelson**

130

thedral, and hundreds more collected outside the doors. They had all come after a long and serious Lenten fast. Inside the church, tinder had been laid for the Easter fire. When the bishop arrived, he stood before the tinder and a hush fell over the crowd. They waited for the tinder to ignite. Coptic Christians claim that this happens by spontaneous combustion and only if the celebrant has prayed and properly fasted. When the tinder glowed and then burst into flame, a roar came from the crowd, and they cheered the new and holy fire. Then in the darkened church, the fire was passed from person to person. When it reached the doors, they were opened, and the fire was passed to the crowds outside. A new roar rose from those outside as they saw and accepted the holy fire.

## OUR EASTER

Our own Easter fires must have something of that same sacred, breathless, will-it-ignite quality about them. That is why the old rubrics require that the fire be lit from flint and steel. There has to be the breathless quality of chance, the realness of flame and fire passed amongst us, the cheers of relief and success. For that, we hear chanted *Lumen Christi!* We have that wonderful word *Alleluia*, that ritual cry of joy and relief which we have not heard for over six, Lenten weeks. For that we sing the *Gloria* and ring the church bells. Our church has no bells so everybody brings a bell from home. At the intonation of the *Gloria*, out come the muffled bells; then we ring them like mad—lots of little bells, some big bells, dinner gongs, even a cow bell. At that point we have to at least smile, and the children just laugh aloud.

A token fire, lit in a little bowl at the back of the church where no one hears or sees or smells it—flicked into existence quickly with the aid of lighter fluid and a cigarette lighter—is no archetypal fire. It has lost power. An *Alleluia* that has neither been sung in a glorious number of ways all year nor then denied, and then pealed forth again in the midst of the Easter night has lost impact and meaning.

## BURIAL OF THE ALLELUIA

I remember a time when I was preparing a class of children for Lent. All year at morning prayers, we had sung psalms and *Alleluias*. And now I explained that that cheerful word would be de-

**Christian Formation of Children**

nied us. We wouldn't say or sing it even once for the six weeks of Lent. What could we do with that word so that it was out of our reach? The children, seated in a ring around me, began to chatter. Some made motions with their hands of pressing it down. "Bury it!" was one suggestion. "Yah! Bury it!" they agreed. Without knowing it, they were suggesting a ritual burial of the *Alleluia* that was indeed a known and common practice in other times and in other parts of the world. Given the chance, the children responded directly and simply from the collective unconscious. So we got out large sheets of paper and each wrote the word large and beautifully, every letter decorated with designs and flowers and joyful colors and signs of spring. We sang all the *Alleluias* we knew for the last time. Then they folded their papers and took these home, put them in jars and found a place in their garden to bury them until Easter.

This little ritual, which rose quite spontaneously from my students, almost backfired. It happened that two of the children, a brother and a sister, were out digging their holes when their father arrived home from work. He saw them burrowing amongst his daffodils, one in the front garden and one in the back, and he demanded to know what they were up to. The boy offered that they were burying a word—a word that he couldn't say any more—their teacher said so. "What word? Did you learn it from her?" "Sure, of course!" The girl wouldn't make the story any clearer. "It's a very special word and we're not going to say it, not until Easter and then . . . ." But apparently by that time the father was in the house demanding an explanation from me on the phone. When I explained, he was not only relieved but delighted and resolved to join the children in a resurrection of the *Alleluia* on Easter morning as a part of the family egg-hunting ceremonies.

DOING WITHOUT FIRE

In my parish, now, there are families who have made it a practice during the days from Good Friday to Easter, to do without fire, that is without anything that requires a flame, like cooked food. Some even give up hot showers so that when the sacred fire of the Easter night is kindled and blessed and praised and sung to, it can be brought home again by a candle in a jar. The holy fire is

**Gertrud Mueller Nelson**

used to renew the pilot lights and kindle a fresh fire in the cleaned-out hearth. We learned that certain Native Americans, the Incas, and the ancient Chinese have such a festival in the spring, and they too receive a sacred fire from the shaman. The Incas, for instance, wait for their shaman to receive it. He catches it by means of a crystal directly from the Sun, then distributes it to every household that has been cold and dark and without cooked food for three days.

I can remember a blustery, rainy Easter night where parishioners had witnessed the successful lighting of the Easter fire against all odds. Once inside the church, we felt blessed and victorious with our little flames.

After services and after the Easter feastings and greetings were over, we all trekked out to our cars in a blowing rain trying to get our little flames as far as the car. Two young men approached us from the parking lot. They told us they'd gotten all the way to their van, and in slamming the door, their candle had gone out. They wanted to share in our flame and wanted to warn us that even closing the car door was a danger to getting our fire home successfully. We shared our flame, crept into our car, and, sure thing, when we closed the door—even though we were ever so careful—our candle went out!

The two young men had not driven off yet. They were sitting in their van watching to see how we would fare. Again, they shared their light with us, and we had to laugh with joy and satisfaction at our fire-light fraternity. As they drove off, the next family came knocking at our car window needing a light from our candle. We gave them a tip on how to close the car door and save the flame. Up and down the parking lot in the wind and the rain we heard the families laughing and calling out as flames went out and were rekindled. "Wow," said one of our kids. "This fire *is* magic! I know what you mean—you can give it away and you never lose; it only makes more." In the *Exsultet*, we had just sung "*A flame divided but undimmed.*" And here, we were experiencing it in some very graphic way.

We also carry home the newly blessed water in a special bottle and use that water to bless our Easter foods the next morning. We save that water, in its very beautiful bottle, to use throughout the coming year: to bless those in the family who may be ill, or traveling, or taking an important exam. It blessed little children at bed-

**Christian Formation of Children**

time. It blessed the new car, the seeds that go into the ground in the spring, the Advent wreath, the Christmas tree. Over and over, we are reminded of our Baptism into this community of believers and of how our membership has an impact on everything that happens to us, no matter how everyday the situation. This is not superstition, not magic, but rather a rite to engage and heighten the awareness of the moment and call God's grace into the situation.

When the Church denies us something, like the use of *Alleluia*, or encourages a fast or when it asks us to wait during Advent, too often, for too long, we have viewed these periods of denial or longing as a punishment and as masochistic. In reality, we can come to see that periods of denial really help us to experience life's gifts with greater joy and awareness. I think that the Church, even though we have a tendency to forget this, is a great teacher of joy. Indeed, there is no crown without a cross. But this is the balance we must create in our lives.

It is in this spirit that we go forth to be true to the themes which the Church year offers us and which match and point up and ratify our own most human experiences. Let us bring ritual back into our personal lives, into our families and classrooms, into our parish festivities. For ritual, symbol, and myth is that expression which marries what is divine with what is most human in us. The making of a ceremony or a ritual is not just something that we do to or for our children. Certainly we have already had the profound experience of doing something which began as a "project to include the children," and discovered that our own involvement touched *us* deeply. The symbolic life requires us to strip down to what is basic and essential in us, and there we come upon the child within. Unless we become as little children, unless we involve ourselves just as directly as a child will who digs in the sand, who carries his Easter fire home, who blows out the candles on his birthday cake, we cannot enter into the kingdom of heaven. Ritual is the place where our humanity crosses with the transcendent. Ritual is the place where we *find* faith.

To end our considerations of the mythic, the ritual, and the symbolic life, I would like to share with you something that was introduced to me when I was in the second grade. It was given to me in a little book which I still have and still value. It was something which was not so lofty that it was over my head. It was

**Gertrud Mueller Nelson**

something so real and direct that I never outgrew it. That is symbolic life at its best.

Romano Guardini, the classic liturgist, in his superb and timeless little booklet, *Sacred Signs,* which was written in 1930, gives us a meditation appropriate for a sign and ritual that we have always available to us—the Sign of the Cross. I would like to end with his short meditation. It is both so profound and so simple that it speaks to people of any age. It is the sort of meditation we can do with our children. It is the sort of thing that we can do for ourselves. This is what he says:

> You can make the sign of the cross, and make it rightly. Nothing in the way of a hasty waving of the hand, from which no one could understand what you are doing—no, a real sign of the cross: slow, large, from forehead to breast, and from one shoulder to the other. Don't you feel that it takes in the whole of you? Gather up all thoughts and all feeling into this sign, as it goes from forehead to breast; pull yourself together, as it goes from shoulder to shoulder. It covers the whole of you, body and soul; it gathers you up, dedicates you, sanctifies you.

> Why? Because it is the sign of the whole man and the sign of redemption. On the Cross our Lord redeemed all persons. Through the Cross He sanctifies the whole person, to the very last fibre of his being.

> That is why we cross ourselves before our prayers, so that the sign may pull us together and set us in order, may fix thoughts, heart and will in God. After prayers we cross ourselves, so that what God has given us may stay with us. In temptation, that it may strengthen us; in danger, that it may protect us; when a blessing is given, that the fullness of life from God may be taken into our soul, and may consecrate all in it and make it fruitful.

> Think of this when you make the sign of the cross. It is the holiest sign there is. Make it carefully, slowly; make a large one, with recollection. For then it embraces your whole being, body and soul, your thoughts and your will, imagination and feeling, doing and resting; and in it all will be strengthened, stamped, consecrated in the power of Christ, in the name of the Holy Trinity (Romano Guardini, *Sacred Signs,* Sheed and Ward, London 1930).

Portions of this paper are taken from the author's *To Dance with God: Family Ritual and Community Celebration.* Mahwah, N.J.: Paulist Press, 1986.

**Christian Formation of Children**

Robert W. Hovda

# Liturgy Forming Us in the Christian Life

It sounds so easy, doesn't it—so simple, so natural: "Liturgy forming us in the Christian life." But we know very well that we do not yet have, in most parishes or local churches, a community enabled to worship by experiences of conversion, catechumenate, rites of Christian initiation and their nurturing weaning from individualism and privatism to the solidarity and mutual love of the body of Christ. The priority which the Rite of Christian Initiation of Adults (RCIA) and the Sunday liturgy should enjoy on the agenda of every parish, every local church, is still a dream, still a vision full of hope and promise but terribly far from where we are.

So our gratitude for being part of a remarkable and wonderful time in the history of the Church also carries its sorrows and its cross. For when we see something good, when we are captured by a vision, we want to see results. We are not so attracted to the reforms and changes in ourselves which are the conditions, the *sine qua non* of any results at all. That we, the baptized and presently committed, are the Church and that the liturgy is not only our inheritance but our doing, our common ministry—these fundamental notions, these absolutely fundamental convictions have to be more than talk at conferences. They have to be parts of our experience, the experience of all of us.

Our kind of group suffers a special difficulty, I think, in trying to understand the seriousness of the ecclesial pathology indicated by the theme of this conference. Are not most of us here engaged, on a fairly regular basis, in roles of leadership, specialized ministry, in a Sunday assembly whose common ministry is not yet appreciated? And don't these roles, these functions, tend to make us overly optimistic about our progress? Whether we are clergy, musicians, ushers, readers, acolytes, Eucharistic ministers, or serving the rest of the assembly in some other specialized task, I recommend that we participate in the Sunday liturgy without portfolio, divested of our specialized functions, as often as we can. Only then can we fully appreciate the situation of most Catholics on Sunday—not only the unconscious and negative impressions communicated by the assembly's leaders but also the terrible psychological distance which our top-heavy and clericalist habits place between the liturgical action and the people.

We overlook what all our rites assume: that in both worship and mission it is the Church *as a whole* that is the primary minister. After centuries of obsession with the Church's universal aspects, it is a difficult lesson to learn. Members who had been satisfied to consider themselves customers at any one of the local outlets of an international entity were suddenly invested, after the council, with a dignity and responsibility quite foreign to the passive consumerism with which they had become comfortable.

Presiders and other worship leaders, especially the clergy, must see themselves *first* as members of the Sunday assembly. One cannot serve appropriately in any role of specialized ministry unless one is consciously and in a heartfelt manner a part of the community—not coming at it from above but aware of the radical egalitarianism of baptism and Eucharist. That is why our initiation rites clearly say that all initiates, all members of the Church, are called and equipped to "carry out the mission of the entire people of God in the church and in the world" (RCIA, Gen. Intro. #2). There is no implication at all that Church affairs are the province of the clergy and the world's affairs are the province of the rest of the Church. Quite the opposite. Both worship and mission are tasks common to us all. We have a distinction of roles of the sort required by human social activity, but the whole work of the Church is the common responsibility of all the initiated. The bishop, priest, or other minister who is preoccupied with self, who is not visibly and really a worshiper and a member of the worshiping community, who relishes authority, imagines self the host, and has a proprietary attitude toward the word of God—that poor minister is such a flagrant anomaly that no grace of gesture or of speech can compensate. Body language communicates this devastating attitude even when our words are what they should be.

One other point in this long preface: I'm sure the word "spirituality" means different things to different people, but I suspect in almost every case the explanation or definition will uncover a personal element, something that has to do with that person, something in which that person is involved. The word has a personal sound to it. On the other hand, while liturgy is a much less ambiguous word, the same search among Christians for a definition or explanation, I suspect again, will reveal almost no consciousness of personal involvement. It will be explained or defined as something "out there," an object, not *our action*. In fact, we give ourselves and our pathology away every time by contrasting liturgy with what we call "personal prayer." We mean "private prayer," of course, which *is* different from liturgy. But for us the communal is not personal, and that is a deadly defect. Liturgy cannot be private, but it *must* be personal, both personal *and* communal. Because it is *our* experience it is also *my* experience. Our language and our categories cut us off from so much in the world and in our lives. No formation is possible if we let this happen with liturgy.

Writing in The Liturgical Conference's membership journal, Virginia Sloyan comes to our aid, voicing the experience of the greater part of the assembly at Sunday Mass:

> Convincing us that we exercise a crucial role in the liturgical celebration, that we in effect *are* the celebration, cannot be achieved by verbal persuasion. . . . Sunday after Sunday we nourish a hope, faint and often unfulfilled, that our worship will take us to places of beauty and meaning we do not normally inhabit, places we have helped to create, places we will return from, refreshed and whole. "Where there is no vision," Proverbs reminds us, "the people perish" (29:18). We come to this setting to hear the sacred story and pray the great prayer with sisters and brothers, hoping to feel enlarged, expansive, full of praise, better than we are, knowing this is the way God sees us in Christ Jesus.
>
> We cannot be trained to listen creatively, respond enthusiastically, offer warmhearted peace greetings or form images that will delight and challenge throughout the week, any more than a child can be trained to express exhilaration at finding a beautifully wrapped package under the Christmas tree, only to learn that it conceals socks and underwear. The utilitarian has little interest for a child and no place in liturgy. The gifts that planners and ministers provide for us, their co-worshipers, must dazzle in their splendor. These persons are artists, who will have the highest respect for the art forms they render. Gifts of like quality will be given by us in return. We will act symbolically and ritually because that will be the only appropriate response (*Liturgy*, Vol. 6, no. 4, 14, 17).

Sloyan is saying the experience must *elicit* this kind of active participation, this kind of desire for formation; it isn't created by

**Robert W. Hovda**

lecturing. Yet the growing gap between the rich and the poor in our country is nothing compared to the gap between the liturgy as it is talked about in conferences and the liturgy as it is experienced in the Sunday assembly.

So those first questions in the announcement of this conference are not merely rhetorical: "Have the dreams of the liturgical pioneers been realized? Is the liturgy truly 'the summit toward which the activity of the Church is directed . . . the fount from which all her power flows'? Is active participation 'the primary and indispensable source' from which the faithful are deriving 'the true Christian spirit'?" Present company excepted, an honest answer to all three questions can be nothing but a resounding "No," partly because it took more than a few decades for us to get the way we are and it's going to take more than the few decades we have seen since the council to get us more clearly, responsibily, maturely, experientially on the right track. But that is only part of the problem. We can complain all we want about people not being formed by the liturgy which should form them, and our complaints will continue to be futile. The other part of the problem is the part we can do something about, especially since most of us here are leaders, influential in the faith community.

What can we do today to make the Sunday liturgy the kind of experience that elicits, draws, demands personal involvement, and thereby is a fount of formation? Let me simply touch on five areas of attention and growth with regard to liturgical celebration that have everything to do with "the true Christian spirit"; I assume that is what we mean by "spirituality." 1. We must become fluent in the symbol language of worship, 2. Cherish the unfinished, pilgrim nature of the Church, 3. "Let tomorrow take care of itself" (Matt 6:34), and 4. Make the world your home and your project. 5. Absorb the sources for the sake of activating our imaginations.

1. *Become fluent in the symbol language of worship.* By "symbol language," I mean both the biblical word—which is poetic and symbolic compared to our factual prose—and the sacramental acting-out of our orientation to the one true God and therefore to God's liberating and reconciling will for all of us. Bible and sacrament together come to life in this deed of the Sunday assembly and in the light of the signs of our own times. The entire action is symbol. And every part of that action must be done so beauti-

fully, so carefully, so worshipfully, so intelligibly, and with such appeal to all our senses, that it commands attention and involvement.

Specialists in the field tell us that our verbal efforts are a very small part of the communications process. They suggest that more is communicated in unspoken and nonverbal ways—by expression, gesture, body language, choreography, music, and the other arts in symbolic ways that touch not just our reason, like points one, two and three, but also our memories, imaginations, senses, all the levels of our complex beings. This is true in all communication, but above all in worship where we deal with the mystery of God, the inexpressible, the Holy One at whom our words can only aim, never capture. Our verbal efforts and formulas are inevitably imprisoned in a particular time, place, language, culture, situation. The symbol language of liturgy, on the other hand, is universal and comprehensive, some kind of huge human reservoir into which we all tap: person, earth, water bath, bread and wine, common table, rock, fire, music, incense, oil massage, kiss of peace, foot washing, procession and dance, icon, and all the rest. We don't have to learn this language; it is natural to us. But in our technical, scientific, pragmatic, capitalist culture, we do have to make special efforts to remain sensitive to it, to revive it, to become skilled in it, fluent, by opening up the symbols to feed our experience and quicken our spirits—opening them up from the shriveled and desiccated state into which our Church history and our Western culture have conspired to allow them to lapse. That communication is on the level, the deep level, of the meaning of life, not on the superficial level of a blueprint or a party line or a little list of do's and don't's.

In a moment of reaction against reform, like the one we are presently enduring, we have to keep reminding ourselves of this, lest we forget our catholicity and become sectarian, narrow partyliners. The late William Lynch pointed to the danger:

> This drive toward common movement and ritual . . . is one of the most powerful movements of the human soul. If it is choked off and denied on the deepest and religious levels of existence, as indeed it has been, it will concentrate the whole of itself on the most superficial levels of life, the immediately social, and will end in becoming an absolute, a parody of itself and of its own dignity. Whereas, if we were really united at the bedrock of our natures,

**Robert W. Hovda**

140

most of the pressures toward the kind of conformism that we all really hate would be enormously lessened (*Christ and Apollo: The Dimensions of the Literary Imagination*, New York: Mentor-Omega, 1963, 175).

The message, the good news communicated in liturgy, is that we are forgiven; made new persons; identified with Christ, the beloved of God; enabled to signal the reign of the one true God with its twin characteristics of justice and peace or liberation and reconciliation or freedom and solidarity or whatever other synonyms one chooses—the two inseparable aspects of salvation. Liturgy is the sign, the new Jerusalem, showing us as much as possible what that reign is like. In liturgy we act it out, setting the vision of faith, God's design and will for creation—"Your kingdom come. Your will be done on earth as in heaven."—in the midst of a status quo still full of oppression and division. The message, the Good News, is of the reign of that one-only God who makes us free and one and calls us to bring about liberation and solidarity in our world. Only in God can that justice and peace flourish together, inseparably. Without God, we are easy targets for other masters, other powers, and our distinctions and variety, instead of being enrichment, rear walls of prejudice and hate.

The symbolic action of worship puts us in a situation as like the reign of God as we can imagine, transports us into the kind of world we are supposed to be creating. It doesn't tell us how—no blueprints, no party line, no detailed instructions or maps as to the immediate steps and ways—but it gives us the vision, with two obvious corollaries: in dialogue with the rest of the world and its gifts and with our gifts of faith, mind, imagination, technical achievement, we have to find ways to bring about the liberation and the solidarity of all in the human family, and those ways must be appropriate, good, holy at every point, else they betray the vision.

We don't need more words in liturgy. Frequently, we have too many now. What we need desperately is to do the liturgy with such love and appreciation of its symbol langauge that it cannot help being an experience for all participants: the worship space beautiful, awesome, hospitable; seating for common action and the possibility of seeing each other's faces; making reverence for every person present a felt experience; readings proclaimed so that no

**Forming the Christian Life**

one misses a word; baptism a real water bath at the hands of a caring community; real bread, real wine presented and prayed over as tokens of our thanksgiving and our self-offering in Christ, the body and blood of the Word-made-flesh, broken and poured out and shared from common plates and common cups to make us one; professional music leadership with first-rate repertoire for choir and good strong hymnals for the whole assembly; specialized ministers who know how to vest and sit and stand and walk and gesture as worshipers and leaders of worship and servants of the rest of the assembly.

Doing the liturgy well also means letting go of all those habits that make the liturgy look like an object, a thing, rather than our action, our celebration of what our lives mean when joined to Christ. We need a tabernacle of reservation in a separate room for private prayer and communion for those who cannot come to Mass, with absolutely no traffic to or from it during the liturgy; the abolition of Mass stipends everywhere, so that our intentions may be integrated in the General Intercessions on Sunday, where they belong; the local Church gathered as much as possible into one assembly, rather than having multiple assemblies for a community that need not be divided. Always in our talk of Church it must be *we*, not *they*: the sacraments of initiation and our present commitment must mark us rather than the minor distinctions we need and have in the various specialized ordained or commissioned ministries within the body.

If all of us together are the body of Christ, no one of us is the whole Christ. So Catholic tradition tells us that even the youngest, the most powerless, the least promising among us has an approach to faith, a gift, an insight to contribute to the common life and hoped-for consensus of the Church. It is a messy process—all these gifts coming together, not always agreeing, sanding the rough spots and edges off each other. It is not as simple as dictatorship or monarchy or democracy, but it is the biblical and ecclesial way, the way of orthodoxy in our tradition. That is how we grow.

2. *Cherish the unfinished, pilgrim nature of the Church.* Whether we speak of our regular Sunday assembly or our diocese or the national Church or the Churches in communion with the Roman Church around the world, we are speaking of a pilgrim entity un-

Robert W. Hovda

finished, incomplete, in process, like the world and all creation. Beginning with the first rites of initiation, the Church is a pilgrim, with faith's vision of God's reign and faith's prescription that our means and steps must be good ones but with the journey left pretty much up to our wits and in our hands. Even the vision is always communicated according to our capacity to receive it at any given time and place.

You and I can accept and love ourselves much more easily if we understand that we are individually, also, pilgrims and un-finished, always in process, capable of loving better, knowing more, doing with great effectiveness than we love and know and do right now. If we didn't think we could grow in some way, achieve something more, make some bit of progress, life would be intolerable. In the same way, we can take the ugliness of the Church in so many of our aspects as long as we realize that as Church, too, progress is possible; clearer vision, new and better insights into the meaning of the classic gospel and its symbol lan-guage are more than possible. They are what the journey is about. The liturgy makes it clear: death and new life, dying to what op-presses and divides in order to inch the world along toward the freedom of all of us—without which none of us is really free—and the oneness of all humanity—without which all are fragmented and divided. Our ecclesial history and experience prove this: they reveal an astounding progress in faith consciousness and con-science over the millennia despite the fact that from the viewpoint of my brief life or yours the development appears so desperately slow.

But we don't like the risk, the modesty, the patience, the uncer-tainty of being a pilgrim very much. So the Church on its deepest level, the level of its vision and its liturgy, stimulates progress, offers us the dynamic of evolution, makes us part of a living tradi-tion to which we contribute. At the same time, on its practical, daily-life level, the Church tends to fight progress, sometimes more—as in this particular moment of sectarian, narrow reaction— and sometimes less—as in the first decades after the council—but the tension is always in our life: the vision versus the status quo and the desires of administrators to win the Good Housekeeping Seal of Approval. For both Jews and Christians, this is the pain of accepting the covenant: accepting a vision which is always beckon-ing us on and is never satisfactorily realized, a vision to which we

**Forming the Christian Life**

cannot measure up—one that attracts, pulls us along, inspires, prompts our tiny baby steps but is never captured, never achieved.

Isn't that why repentance is a constant refrain in the Bible and the liturgy? It is not for the reasons we too commonly suppose—to turn us back, make us feel guilty, embarrass us with remembrance of the way we've lived. No, that kind of fruitless introspection is a refusal to accept the saving power of God who has reconciled us in Jesus Christ. Rather, repentance is a call to open up to the guidance of the Spirit into new paths, to become new, to let go of the past. We can't be pilgrims, engage in a journey, a quest, a search, if our eyes are on the rear-view mirror.

Because we had experienced a static period for so long, when Church reform began again in the 60's, it was natural for us to expect that this stirring up of the waters and unsettling of our tranquillized spirits would eventually be over and we could look forward to another period of quiet. But we learned more from the council than we bargained for. What appeared at first like a period of reform that would have an end as well as a beginning now has to be accepted as the only way of life to which the Church has any claim. We must always be reforming. Reform is not a medicinal dose taken to return us to normalcy. Reform *is* normalcy for a pilgrim people. We have opened the windows, and our ecclesiastical second thoughts—so evident today—fortunately lack the muscle to close them again. Pilgrim we remain.

3. *"Let tomorrow take care of itself"* (Matt 6:34). These words of Jesus may be his most difficult prescription. He tells us that the arena of moral life is today and only today—what we are and do today. But that's not for us. We want results. We want tomorrow, next year, next decade to be our arena. We are like Thomas Becket's protectors. Remember the words that Eliot puts in Becket's mouth: "Unbar the door! You think me reckless, desperate and mad. You argue by results, as this world does, to settle if an act be good or bad" (*Murder in the Cathedral* in *The Complete Poems and Plays*, New York: Harcourt Brace & World, 1971, 211).

We argue by results. We overlook today, the act, the immediate decision, and find ourselves doing the most horrifying things and committing the ugliest and most vicious deeds because the conventional wisdom says that only in this way will we make a better

**Robert W. Hovda**

144

tomorrow. Tomorrow is our alibi. Our election campaigns are a case in point. It is too easy to blame the mass media and the pollsters for the fact that voting now seems less an expression of what we want in government and more like the placing of a bet on a presumed winner. For the media and the polls only give us what they think we want: the results before the cause, the outcome before the action, the end before the means. That way we aren't responsible. We have been informed about how it will come out; therefore, we don't have to decide anything about the state of the nation, the priority to be attached to our various problems, and we don't have to exercise our wits and our imaginations to make sure that we have parties and candidates who will offer real alternatives. All we have to decide is whether we want to be with the winners or with the losers. And we know quite well what the conventional wisdom tells us about winners and losers.

So we don't get excited about the experience of our Sunday liturgical assembly either because *ex opere operato* we're just trading that hour off anyway for a future reward tomorrow. Nothing else matters but the grace. And that defies measurement, so we're safe. For the same reason, we build up our arsenals of unspeakable devastation and annihilation because they will create peace tomorrow. And we support and connive with an economic system that creates more and more poor people, with a greater and greater gap between them and the obscenely wealthy, because we have persuaded ourselves that some day all of us can be obscene.

But Jesus says *today* is the day. Jesus says the only way to prepare for the future is to live the reign of God today, as totally as our vision can manage. If today is what today can be, with the best we can bring to it, then tomorrow will take care of itself. If the step I make today, the deed I do, the conversation I carry on, the way I relate to all the sisters and brothers is good, peaceful, loving, just, then I am doing more for the future than someone whose eyes and heart are on results, on tomorrow or the next century. Dorothy Day was fond of quoting St. Therese: "All the way to heaven is heaven. . . ." It's easy to plan for salvation after death when there is no contest. The squeeze is today, this time, this place.

The philosopher Kierkegaard put it another way:

There is only one end—the genuine Good; and only one means:
this is to be willing to use only those means which genuinely are

good. . . . One is not responsible for whether one reaches the goal within this world of time. But without exception one is eternally responsible for the kind of means one uses. And when one will only use those means which are genuinely good, then, in the judgment of eternity, one is already at the goal (*Purity of Heart Is to Will One Thing . . .*).

Our job, then, if we are serious about liturgy forming us for the Christian life, is to make it experiential today for all of us—not to aim at some future time or to plan a "good liturgy" for the kids. Our job is to take that frequently dreadful and *pro forma* Sunday Eucharistic assembly and do it so attractively, so dazzlingly, that it grabs our insides.

4. *Make the world your home and your project.* Jewish and Christian biblical and liturgical tradition is distinctive on the point of its worldliness and earthiness. The faith community exists to be salt, light, leaven in and with and for the rest of the world—the only world we have—so we have to be part of it. Besides, we *need* the rest of the world. We share the world's discoveries, inventions, development, growth as signs of the times, another source along with our faith sources. But you know as well as I do that we have contrary habits, ingrained habits, bad habits of separating ourselves as Church out of the world, creating a kind of Church world all by itself, independent, pure, untouched by what myopic types see as all that "secular" mess out there. Open eyes, of course, can discern "secular mess" inside the Church as well as outside, but we ignore that patent fact.

So we must resist every temptation to separate the Church and its worship from the rest of the world or to devise a "spirituality" that is private and self-indulgent. Our call is to be part of our world, first, and after that is clearly established, then to be a servant-witness to the rest of the world. Biblical faith sees the world as epiphany of God. The Church's purpose, therefore, is not to isolate its members nor to consume their lives and their time nor to duplicate all human services and fill our datebooks with Church activities, but rather, in the midst of the world, to inspire and orientate us for a life elsewhere. The temptation to be a ghetto, a fortress, a tropical island, an escape has been powerful and needs to be rooted out of us for the sake of both worship and mission.

**Robert W. Hovda**

Brevity sometimes requires caricature. In our history, when whole countries were called "Christian" and when conversion and baptism consequently faded into the landscape, we as Church became, more or less, merely the pious face of the society. Just as our sacraments shriveled up in liturgical decadence and rigidity in that period, so our morality shriveled up into the relatively private sphere of sex because power and money were now on our side, and people don't argue with those on their side. The institutions, governments, systems we had not feared to confront earlier now favored us, so we turned the full brunt of our moral indignation on the individual.

Now that we are no longer privileged with a high social status, perhaps we can regain a morality closer to the gospel we preach, indeed part of the gospel we preach—less private and less individual. We can't get blood out of a turnip and we can't get excited, warm, experiential liturgical celebrations out of people who are unconcerned about the economic and political oppression and division in the world.

The rapid advances in the world of the last century correspond to the promise of the Bible. The biblical vision of one world, one humanity, is already close although we haven't learned how to deal with it, how to organize our world for it. But now we know that institutions once regarded as unchangeable fate or destiny are our creations; we made them, we keep them in existence, and we can change them. People at large were not aware of this before our time; some still are not. The late Joseph Sittler used to say that what was once the bringing of a glass of water to a thirsty person is now the more complicated and effective prevention of thirst by dealing with systems of obtaining, purifying, and distributing water.

Listen to what an American Russian Orthodox theologian, the late Alexander Schmemann, wrote long ago about this problem:

> Before we gain the right to dispose of the old "symbols," we must understand that the real tragedy of Christianity is not its "compromise" with the world and progressive "materialism," but, on the contrary, its "spiritualization" and transformation into "religion." And religion has thus come to mean a world of pure spirituality, a concentration of attention on matters pertaining to the "soul." Christians were tempted to reject time altogether and replace it with mysticism and spiritual pursuits, to live as Christians

**Forming the Christian Life**

out of time and thereby escape its frustrations, to insist that time has no real meaning from the point of view of the kingdom which is "beyond time." And they finally succeeded. They left time meaningless indeed, although full of Christian "symbols." And today they themselves do not know what to do with these symbols. For it is impossible to "put Christ back into Christmas" (for example) if Christ has not redeemed—that is, made meaningful—time itself (*For the Life of the World*, New York: National Student Christian Federation, 1963, 32).

5. *Absorb the sources for the sake of activating your imaginations.*
Until the uniqueness of that primary and indispensable source, the liturgy—especially the Sunday assembly—becomes strong and experiential enough to impinge significantly on the consciousness of those of us who still participate in it, we cannot be surprised that the spirituality of many is fabricated from the very privatism, individualism, and angelism which the gospel is designed to cure.

The poetry of the Bible and the body language of the sacraments and other liturgies together constitute the symbol that communicates the basic principles of any faithful spirituality: our freedom and our oneness. Liturgy communicates our freedom by orientating our worship to God alone, our oneness by naming God our common source and source of our commonness, as well as by the figure of the meal shared with Christ as Head of the table, the body. Like other symbols, liturgy communicates this in myriad ways to every level of our beings, many of those levels too subtle for our consciousness or our articulation.

It is in that symbol, that liturgy, that we have to plant our hooks and find our guidance. Putting the classic communication of the Sunday assembly together with what we can discern as the signs of our own times, we have the basic material and environment for the formation of conscience. The strokes are bold, classical, comprehensive, seminal, non-specific, as liturgy in its basic structure must be so that it can serve all times, all places. So there is a clear distinction between the beliefs that constitute the basis of our unity in faith, on the one hand, and the party lines, platforms, or political and economic programs we human beings have to figure out in the light of two phenomena: our growth in understanding of God's revelation and the constantly changing signs of the times. The tools, the ways, the means are left up to our imaginations, skills, and progress.

**Robert W. Hovda**

Between the basic sources of our formation and the daily task of inching our world along toward the justice and peace of God, are all of us as interpreters of these sources. Since the Church has no consumers, no body of mere clients or patients, no passive membership—in spite of our fondness for the word "laity"—we are all interpreters of those basic sources and the signs of the times. We also have official, trained, talented interpreters to help us. To maintain a clear distinction between the sources and the interpreters is not to discount the latter; it is only to indicate there is a real and vital difference.

I said before that we as Church both fuel or stimulate human progress and fight against it. We do it all the time, and we always have, even though it formerly was not on the front page or the television every day. The fueling is on the level of symbol, sources. The fighting against is often, though not always, on the level of administrators and interpreters. We study the interpretations, and we learn from one another. But the sources continue to be the sources, unique in their authority. It is our great variety, our different gifts and approaches and cultures that enrich the processes of interpretation and demand a constant reconciling search for ecclesial consensus, or what tradition calls *sensus ecclesiae*. That is a long, time-consuming process.

We have to watch out for our current culture which wants headlines, quick answers, instant gratification. Christians, at least the more serious ones, used to have to go to the sources, the Sunday assembly, because there was nowhere else to go. Now we just read the papers or turn on the television and the answers are there from media-wise popes, bishops, theologians, and catechists even before we've asked a question. And the answers—for the media's time is money—are pre-packaged, wrapped up, definitive, neat and tidy. Christians who used to grow up and become adults, with consciences that struggle with questions, are now able to remain children forever, spoon fed.

When we see the kind of rapid consciousness-raising we are seeing in our century, on the level of our sources we are all in favor of it; on the level of our daily life as Church we frequently oppose it. For example, the movement for the liberation of women—and men—from the stereotypes imposed by historical patterns of male power and domination or the similar movements among minorities of color or class or sexual orientation or handicaps, or the new

**Forming the Christian Life**

human consciousness hailed by the Second Vatican Council for taking the world in hand rather than merely being victimized by it are all developments spawned and encouraged by the liturgy's biblical message even while frequently opposed by Church leaders.

If, on the level of interpretation, we run into difficulties because the world has been otherwise for so long, because, in Jesus' words, we have nullified God's word for the sake of our traditions (Matt 15:6-10; Mark 7:1-13) and made dogmas out of human precepts, we must let our sources work on us and make ourselves at home on that deeper, fundamental level of the Church's life. If we do this, we will find ourselves emerging from the darkness of prejudice and privilege into the light which, without discrimination, reveals basic equality and the different gifts of different persons, sexes, classes, colors, cultures as things we need to complete us, to fill our empty spots, to enrich our lives, rather than as threats to our illusions of superiority.

I hope these thoughts about our sources in the liturgy and their formative relation to our spirituality have a unity as obvious to my readers as it is in my mind because it is the sources rather than the interpreters that stimulate and activate imagination. And we need imagination, lots of it! We have to stop being afraid of our imaginations. They are great gifts of God. More than any other human faculty, imagination frees us from the heavy hand of habit, from our pet formulas, and our status quo so that we can envision new possibilities, new steps toward God's reign. Harvey Cox writes:

> Why do we need imagination? We need it because the substance of the universe of thought is just too changing and too complex to be appropriated in a merely rational manner. Therefore, it is the job of the imagination to operate a "dialectic of the real and the possible." Without imagination, "discursive thought would become incurably crippled in a closed and ossified system" (*The Feast of Fools*, Cambridge: Harvard, 1969, 66).

Jesus, our Savior, struggled against such closed and ossified systems all through his public ministry and on the cross. Pilgrims do not necessarily disregard precedent, but they move ahead nonetheless. A spirituality that has dug up, uncovered, made its own, those sources of Bible and sacrament we have in the liturgy and is therefore ecclesial and of this world rather than private and

**Robert W. Hovda**

angelic, is liberating and reconciling—which is to say, saving. Such a spirituality will be one that elicits different gifts instead of suppressing them, invites new thoughts instead of discouraging them, seeks non-mainstream points of view instead of excluding them, cultivates imagination in everyone instead of trying to freeze us where we are, or were. Although this may seem strange to some of the newly awakened and superficially engrossed among us, this is precisely why it is both appropriate and necessary that the liturgical celebration of the Sunday assembly should be symbolic rather than specific—a scriptural-sacramental communication that refuses to lay upon us a blueprint of action, but rather activates our imaginations.

Maria Leonard

## After Sunday—The Work Week, The Marketplace

The celebration of the liturgy is envisioned in the Vatican II Constitution on the Sacred Liturgy as the summit and source of our Christian life and mission. The image is dynamic and powerful. It implies an organic unity in our lives, a wholeness of faith and work in which our day-to-day lives are empowered and shaped by the liturgy. And the liturgy itself is the moment in which we gather our lives together and celebrate who we are in the Lord.

Yet our experience is not always one of wholeness. We find ourselves sturggling to reconcile the dichotomies of work and prayer, secular and sacred, body and soul, world and Church. How do we bring about wholeness in our lives? How do we reconcile these dichotomies? How do we help others recognize and deepen this unity?

MAKING CONNECTIONS
What is it in the liturgy, the Sunday liturgy, which supports us in our work? What are the connections between our faith as expressed in the liturgy and our work in the marketplace? The chal-

**Work Week and Marketplace**

lenge of making these connections has prodded me for a long time. About thirty years ago, I resigned from my job as secretary with a Fortune 500 company in downtown Manhattan and became a postulant in a religious community. I chose a community which taught only religion—no math or history or nursing for me, just direct ministry and prayer, of course.

After donning the postulant's dress, I was given my work assignment: the laundry. The first morning after being introduced to Lauds and Prime chanted in Latin, we celebrated Mass, ate breakfast in silence, and then reported to our assigned duties. A novice carefully instructed me in the intricacies of ironing coifs, boiling white stockings, and starching collars. Her summary remark before setting me loose to attack a pile of laundry was "Remember, your work here is just as important as the time you spend in chapel praying." That remark has been the cause of much reflection these past thirty years. While a member of the religious congregation, I often struggled with the pull between active ministry and the more mundane responsibilities of community living.

When I left the religious congregation, I accepted a job with the YMCA. My responsibilities were to develop programs for supervisors in business and industry. The goal of these programs was to train managers to be competent, efficient, and more humane. I thought of my work as a ministry, and that was easy to do in a non-profit organization based on Christian values.

Ten years ago, I decided to take the leap into industry. I carefully selected a company that manufactured products which enhance life. Morton Norwich produced and sold the familiar Morton salt packaged in blue containers marked with the little girl and the umbrella. We also made Norwich aspirin, Pepto-Bismol, Glass-Plus, Fantastik, and a host of chemicals, glues, and dyes which ended up in frozen-food packaging, pens, and automobiles. I was proud to work in such a company. I believed that the policies and programs which I developed and implemented enhanced the human dignity of our employees. We initiated a flextime program to allow employees to schedule their own time, a retirement-planning program which helped employees and their spouses identify personal and community resources and begin to plan for their retirement years, and career-development programs to develop strategies to help them achieve fulfillment within the company.

**Maria Leonard**

But in the midst of these benign activities, we sold our phar-
maceutical and household business. I soon found myself in a company which produced missiles, rockets, and bullets, as well as the
propulsion systems for the MX missile and the boosters for the
space shuttle. Everything about the new business was abhorrent
to me and diametrically opposed to my values. Yet there remained
all the people in the corporate office and in two divisions whom I
had grown to know and love. I found that the employees in the
new company were fine human beings, too. After much reflection,
consultation, and discernment, I chose to remain with the company, hoping I could continue to grow and develop within it. I
also believed there was some value in being inside an organization, attempting to change it from within, or at least trying to develop and maintain an environment of respect for the dignity of
all employees.

Within a few months, my resolve was challenged by a group of
peace protesters who urged employees to resign from this company which manufactures death-dealing weapons. Several groups
staged weekly protests, invaded the premises, and expressed their
protest in sometimes bizarre ways. I have come to know many of
them personally. I have been a liaison between them and management several times. As a loyal and respected employee within the
organization, I can raise the issue of peace and disarmament in a
way different from the outsiders. I bring an insider's perspective
to the discussions, but I have basically the same values as the protesters. I have also been able to be supportive to others in the
company who disagree with management on military products. As
I talk with co-workers, I find many who have gone through the
same struggle and are as questioning as I am. I continue to do my
job but find myself continually examining and re-evaluating my
position.

When I think back to the advice of my novice friend, I see my
presence in the company and my work there as just as important
as my worship. It is one part of my unique vocation. Liturgy—
both the actual time of worship and its preparation and
planning—is another part of that same vocation. In the workplace,
I try to bring the peace and justice of the kingdom to the people
and events within my sphere of influence.

In addition to the liturgy, I have been influenced by two recent
documents which have formed and guided my thinking these past

six years: the papal encyclical *Laborem exercens*—On Human Work—published in 1981, and the American bishops' pastoral letter on the economy *Economic Justice for All* published in 1987.

I share my story with you not because it is unique but because it is so similar to the stories of many other people. In the past three years, I have talked with hundreds of people about the relationship of faith and work, about how to be a Christian in the workplace. All of them are seeking a way to become one in Christ, to become whole—whole as persons, whole as a community and a society, and to find meaning in their lives. I will explore three areas which can help us achieve wholeness, this union between faith and work: first, understanding who we are and what we are called to do; second, ways in which the liturgy symbolically supports our total life, but especially life in the marketplace; and third, some practical means of helping people to understand the connections between faith and work.

## I. BAPTISM AND VOCATION: WHO WE ARE

The place to begin is with ourselves. Who are we? We are human beings created in the image of God. Sadly, many of us do not recognize our fundamental dignity. We are the summit of creation, made in God's image with an inalienable dignity that exists prior to any division into race, nation, or gender and prior to human labor and human achievement. This dignity is the source of the solidarity of the human race. In addition, by the gift of God, each of us has become "a new creation in Christ." The American bishops put it this way:

> By faith and Baptism we are fashioned into a "new creation"; we are filled by the Holy Spirit and a new love that compels us to seek out a new profound relationship with God, with the human family and with all created things (*Economic Justice for All*, par. 328).

We are then, before all else, of infinite dignity, made in God's image, and filled with the life of Christ. We are called to a personal responsibility for the world, as co-creators with God and co-redeemers with Christ.

Most people, however, speak of baptism as an event in the past, not as the on-going source of union with Christ and the power underlying all that we do. But baptism doesn't affect just our life of prayer and the sacraments or ministry within the Church. Once

**Maria Leonard**

154

baptized, we never leave those waters. We live in Christ, rooted in Christ, twenty-four hours a day. This is what we must tell people.

At baptisms in our parish, we sing the refrain taken from St. Paul: "You have put on Christ; in Him you have been baptized." We are changed forever; all we touch, like Midas, is touched with magic fingers, fingers guided by the Spirit. We continue to live in the waters of baptism, being watered and nourished, being battered about and dying, but always rising again with Christ. A priest once commented that Easter is too large a mystery for people to deal with. Dying and rising is so foreign to us. How absurd! We experience it daily in losing a job, in retiring, in relocating to another city and in divorce, illness, loss of a friendship. We need only reflect a moment to recognize that mystery in our lives.

Vatican II has brought our baptismal priesthood to the forefront but the emphasis has been on ministry within the Church, and often on liturgical ministry. While we still have a long way to go liturgically, we have barely begun to explore our priesthood in the marketplace and in the family. Fortunately, the Rite of Christian Initiation of Adults has brought a new prominence to baptism in our parishes. Especially during Eastertime, as we are sprinkled with water from the font, we recall once again our dignity: our union with Christ and the refreshment and life that baptism brings.

This renewed understanding of baptism can, perhaps, engender a new view of work. If we ask people about the meaning of work, we will most likely receive a variety of responses: "It's a job which pays the rent." "It's dull and boring." "It's something to do until the weekend." I recently saw a bumper sticker: "A bad day at the beach is better than a good day at work." For those people whose motto is "Thank God it's Friday," work is just a *job*.

Many others are consumed by work; they strive to get ahead and in the process compete with everyone. They relish power and market their talents for gain or greed in order to have "the good life" and the comforts that go with it. For them, work is a *career*.

For yet a third group, work is a *vocation*, a calling to use one's gift to serve others, to promote the common good. These are the people who are personally dedicated to their work, filled with compassion and ideals. They view work as an opportunity to recreate the world, to transform it into our home.

**Work Week and Marketplace**

This is the Christian view of work. It is our vocation; it is an essential part of our lives. We have been given the gift of life, and work is our task. It is more than just a job, although occasionally it is drudgery. It is more than a career, although success and power are not evil in themselves. Work is a means of self-expression, not just for the artist or writer but for the homemaker, typist, bus driver, engineer—all of us. It is the fulfillment of our creative powers. Our work enables us to become more human, more capable of acting intelligently and freely in ways that lead to self-realization. Through our work, as we create ourselves, we are also creating the human community.

Work brings us into relationship with others—our co-workers and others in society—past, present and future. All that exists today—all technology, all factories, all raw materials in nature, all the money in banks—in some sense belongs to us all because it is the result of the work of people who have lived before us. Capital is the heritage we have received from all workers since the beginning of time. We are its stewards, and through our work we are called to use these resources for the benefit of all, for the growth and development of the entire human community, for the common good.

I tested this concept of Christian vocation on two fellow workers, both active Catholics. I asked them whether their faith had any effect on their work. One said, "Yes, it influences the decisions I make and how I treat people." The other said, "I keep them apart." That is the challenge we face: the separation of worship and life. Many people do not see that the two are connected. After a homily about peace or justice, they will remark, "Don't preach politics or economics from the pulpit!" They do not recognize that it is precisely by their work in the midst of the world that they are growing in holiness, that in and through their work they are loving God and their neighbor. The American Bishops describe holiness in this way:

> Holiness is not limited to the sanctuary or to moments of private prayer; it is a call to direct our whole heart and life toward God and according to God's plan for the world. For the laity holiness is achieved in the midst of this world, in family, in community, in friendships, in work, in leisure, in citizenship. Through their competency and by their activity, lay men and women have the vocation to bring the light of the Gospel to economic affairs, "so that

**Maria Leonard**

the world may be filled with the Spirit of Christ and may more effectively attain its destiny in justice, in love and in peace." *(Economic Justice for All,* par. 332).

A Christian vocation, therefore, does not necessarily mean doing anything extra. It is not something tacked on to normal living. It is, rather, our day-to-day activity. If God is revealed most fully in the person of Jesus Christ and all the events of his life, then God is revealed in all the events of our own lives as well, as Christ lives on in us.

## II. LITURGY AND WORK: A VITAL CONNECTION

I once asked a top executive this question, "How does the liturgy support you in your work?" He replied, "I have heard only one sermon in my life that related to my work." That comment brings us to the next point. What is the effect of the liturgy, primarily the Eucharist, on our working lives?

What does work, *as a Christian vocation,* look like? It is all around us. A young woman told me last week that she sees her work as her mission. She is a trainer in a large insurance company which employs many women in low-paying clerical positions; most of them are black, single mothers. She implements training programs which not only develop the technical skills of these women, but also enhance their self-image and inner strength to deal with the many struggles they face daily. Human-resource or personnel managers are often called the "priests" of the corporation. In the Southeast, ministers often hold these positions in small companies. The human-resource person settles conflicts, hears "confessions" or problems, counsels and brings the good news of raises and promotions and the bad news of layoffs and terminations. They also are the advocates for the "little people" in an organization and oftentimes are the lone voice for just and equitable policies.

The building manager in my company lives his job as though it were a vocation although I am sure he would not use that word. For almost thirty-five years he has maintained the building as a home for the employees—supervising the heating, maintenance, mailroom, and cafeteria and organizing parties for special occasions. The entire environment in which we work is comfortable, neat, and efficient because of his dedication and simple, quiet, humble management. He is concerned about our safety and

**Work Week and Marketplace**

health, but he also takes time out to get to know people and their needs. He often advances his own money to young persons who want to use the tuition-refund program but do not have the cash to pre-pay the tuition. He hires minority men and women and encourages their education and advancement. Once, at a time of budget cuts, he offered not to take his salary increase and asked that it be given to someone who needed it more. Recently, I met a woman postal carrier from West Virginia. She trudges up and down streets and sidewalks in a rural town, carrying a heavy bag and delivering mail. She checks on a house where the residents are on vacation, spends extra time talking to a lonely widow. Her job is her vocation.

Jeff Smith—the Frugal Gourmet, television chef, and author of numerous cookbooks—speaks freely about his work as a vocation. Besides teaching people how to cook, he encourages families to share meals together around the table so that they may experience love and unity in one another's company. He often speaks of the symbolism of breaking bread and drinking wine together. He abhors eating standing up or on the run or in the car at a fast-food restaurant with everyone looking forward, not talking to one another.

Several chief executive officers of companies believe they are responsible for providing steady employment and fair wages to employees, an adequate return on investment to shareholders, a quality product and service to customers, taxes paid to the government, and a contribution of five percent of the company's pre-tax income to community organizations.

All of these people, in their own way, bring the peace, justice, and love of Christ to their own sphere of influence in their work, and by so doing are both living out their unique vocation and growing in holiness. They have achieved some measure of wholeness, bringing Gospel values to bear on the totality of their lives.

In a recent address, Archbishop Weakland commented that the most important means of implementing the Economics Pastoral is good liturgy. The bishops describe the connection between worship and the world of work:

> Worship and common prayer are the wellsprings that give life to any reflection on economic problems and that continually call the participants to greater fidelity to discipleship. To worship and pray to the God of the universe is to acknowledge that the healing love

of God extends to all persons and to every part of existence, including work, leisure, money, economic and political power and their
use, and to all those practical policies that either lead to justice or
impede it. Therefore, when Christians come together in prayer, they
make a commitment to carry God's love into all these areas of life
(*Economic Justice for All*, par. 329).

Are we aware of the commitment we make in the liturgy? How
do we carry God's love into life? In *Liturgy and Personality*,
Dietrich Von Hildebrand (London: Longman's Green, 1943) writes
that liturgy shapes and forms our fundamental attitude toward
God and others, that it shapes our affections from which action
flows. However, these affections or attitudes which we find in the
liturgy are for the most part counter to the competitive, capitalistic
environment that we so often find in the marketplace. The liturgy
presents a challenge to us; it calls us to a conversion of heart,
even though this call to conversion takes place on a deeper level
through symbol and ritual and not in the language of rational,
didactic discourse.

How do ordinary Christians talk about the liturgy shaping their
attitudes and behavior? Many of them see the Liturgy of the Word
as having the most obvious role in shaping their lives; however,
there are many other parts of the liturgy whose influence we cannot overlook: the penitential rite, the preparation of gifts, the Eucharistic prayer, the dismissal rite. Those dimensions of the liturgy
which may seem more elusive can, over a period of time, "speak"
powerfully to the worshipping assembly of a reality that goes beyond this-world's experience. Christian liturgy incorporates the
*transcendent*; it appeals to the *senses* and to the *imagination*, to the
fullness of the human person; liturgy is *communal*.

LITURGY OF THE WORD

The Liturgy of the Word, both the readings and the homily, is the
obvious way that the liturgy speaks to most people.

The Old Testament prophets, for example, and Jesus' Sermon
on the Mount challenge materialistic, consumer values and lead to
reflection on lifestyle, attitudes toward money and material things.
In our parish, upwardly mobile yuppies tell of trying to distinguish between "needs" and "wants." They ask, "Do I really
need this latest stereo equipment, this stylish coat? Or am I giving
in to the advertising 'wants' syndrome?"

**Work Week and Marketplace**

Other people question the meaning of success as defined in our culture. Are power and position evil in themselves? Can I be successful and still be a follower of Christ? If I am honest and refuse to do something unethical or to cut corners, will I still get ahead?

A chief executive officer in Minneapolis measures his success by the fact that his company has been in business for over sixty years, continues to offer a needed service and product to customers, has increased its number of jobs from 600 to 3,000 and each year pays a larger dividend to shareholders. At the same time, he manages the company in a participative manner, offering excellent training and development to employees. He is deeply involved in the communities in which the company has plants, encouraging employees to do the same. He provides a variety of benefits to employees: day care, employee-assistance programs, and matching gifts, in addition to the standard health and insurance benefits. His pursuit of justice and the common good has resulted in success, even when measured by economic standards.

Others choose not to play the "power game" in their organizations. They consciously decide to empower others rather than dominate. They are team players, managing in a collaborative manner.

The Gospel calls each of us to define success for ourselves. A career-development program in our company includes a values-clarification exercise to help employees identify what is important to them. All the options are there: achievement, wealth and fame, integrity, religion, inner peace. Through this exercise, participants become aware of how some values conflict with others and of the need to choose behaviors which will satisfy what is really important to them. In the same way, the Gospel challenges us to reflect on our priorities in the light of faith. As a result, we may develop criteria for success which are quite counter cultural.

Some people find the Scripture molding their interest in larger political issues such as peace, military spending, minimum-wage laws, health care for the needy and unemployment. They find creative ways of supporting both the legislation and the candidates who embody the values they believe in. At times, people may be in conflict, wanting to support legislation they believe is just, even though it would negatively affect the profitability of their own company. While the company I work for has a number of government contracts for weapons systems, I consistently write my legis-

**Maria Leonard**

lators to vote against funding for additional military hardware. My beliefs and actions foster discussion and reflection on these issues in the company. Last Christmas, I gave the officers of my company copies of the Economics Pastoral, which resulted in dialogues with several of them. While these may be small ways to influence change, people must determine for themselves what it is possible for them to do and then follow through.

The Scripture shapes our behavior in another more subtle manner. We carry within us certain images from Scripture which can support us in times of confusion or crisis. When faced with a frustrating situation or a difficult decision, we may recall the image of Christ as Good Shepherd. The image brings a sense of peace and well-being, calming our fears and anxieties. As a result, we handle the situation with equity or make the decision with more clarity. While the Scriptures do not give us solutions to problems, they can provide us with the inner resources to respond in faith and trust.

Not only in the Scriptures, but also in the homily there is strong influence to shape attitudes and behavior. When the homilist "listens to the cries of the poor," hears the pains, joys, anger, and frustration of the community, he knows them, can identify with their lives, and can break the bread of the Word in a way that has deep meaning for them.

In one parish, the presiders meet on Monday morning to discuss the readings for the following Sunday. They share insights not only into the meaning of the passages, but also about how these readings apply to the people of the parish at this particular time. These same presiders stand in front of the church to greet people before and after each Mass. When the new pastor arrived, he walked the streets of the entire parish to sense the environment and make-up of the neighborhood. Such efforts help those who preach to know the community to whom the Word will be spoken.

The Prayer of the Faithful is yet another element of the Liturgy of the Word that can be a helpful means of connecting faith and work. Unfortunately, however, poorly written, generic or "canned" prayers are often used instead of carefully crafted prayers, employing evocative language, that keep the needs of the community in mind. If the intercessions are broad as well as specific, the faithful can be led to embrace in prayer and action the needs of a wide variety of people. After praying for the poor, the unemployed, and single mothers at a Sunday celebration, can we refuse to hire one of them on Monday? After praying for the homeless, can we vote against low-income housing for our neighborhood on Tuesday? Of course we can, but not without a greater awareness of the contradiction between our prayers and our behavior.

### PENITENTIAL RITE

The unmentioned plague, the great fear in the business world, is the fear of failure. Failure is absolutely unacceptable. People shy away from the unsuccessful person or the person about to be terminated. No one freely admits errors; excellence is the current motto. The penitential rite, properly celebrated, is a powerful countering force to the fear of failure. We join with others to acknowledge that we are pilgrim sinners and a people in need of conversion. We acknowledge the truth of the situation: that we are not perfect, that we make mistakes. Together, we are accepted by the community and ourselves just as we are, and we move forward, freed. Our acceptance of self and others is not based on success or achievement but on human dignity and the awareness that we are one in our brokenness and our healing. The shuttle disaster was a sign, written in large letters, of people unwilling and fearful to admit that a man-made system was not functioning perfectly. It was a situation filled with fear of failure and hubris. In Irangate, we also found our leaders unable to admit wrongdoing, with ensuing lies and cover-ups. Can we make our reconciliation in the liturgy—in the penitential rite and the greeting of peace, for example—powerful enough to overcome the fears in our hearts?

### PREPARATION OF GIFTS AND DISMISSAL

Two important moments in the liturgy which have a clear relationship to life after Sunday are frequently minimized: the preparation of the gifts and the dismissal. The former is the moment when we gather up our lives, all we have done during the week, and bring them forward that our offerings may be joined to that of Christ.

> *Through your goodness we have this bread to offer,*
> *Which earth has given and human hands have made.*
> *It will become for us the bread of life.*

**Maria Leonard**

*Through your goodness we have this wine to offer,*
*Fruit of the vine and work of human hands.*
*It will become our spiritual drink.*

In this prayer, we declare our total dependence on God for the
gift of our own personal lives and the gift of all creation. We include our work—its creative, joyful elements and its painful
drudgery—that it be united with Christ and transformed so that
we, in our turn, can become the bread of life and the spiritual
drink for our brothers and sisters. This moment puts value on our
past week and looks forward to the transformation of the coming
days.

The preparation of the gifts includes the collection. Many worshippers consider the collection an intrusion into the sacred, and
they are happy when the distraction is over so that they can get
on with their praying. But the collection is a sign of our work and
our lives as well as a symbol of unity with the needy for whom
some of the money will be used. How can we develop the meaning of the collection to demonstrate the unity of work and worship and to balance our tendency toward greed and posses-
siveness? When the collection is brought forward along with the
bread and wine, it becomes an image, a sign—within the Liturgy
of the Eucharist—of the life and the contributions of those who are
gathered around the table.

The Dismissal Rite is the sending-out-on-mission. "As the Father
sent me, so I send you," Jesus told his disciples. Is it because we
are tired or bored that we barely hear these words? In our parish
during Lent, we expanded the dismissal to emphasize that we
were being sent to continue the journey of conversion along with
the catechumens. At each liturgy, we are being sent out to live the
Communion—the solidarity with Christ and his entire body—
which we have just celebrated and received. Our mission is to
bring the peace, the justice, and the love of Christ to the marketplace, to our homes, to our communities, to our leisure, to wherever we are.

THE EUCHARISTIC PRAYER

The Eucharistic Prayer at the heart of the liturgy reminds us that
we have received the gift of life and that we are called to be a
thankful people. One man at work exemplifies for me this spirit of
gratitude. He commented, "Look at the sky, feel the breeze, see

**Work Week and Marketplace**

the world around us. I thank God each day for my life and all of creation, for my job and the people around me." Another co-worker centers her life around Christ, using for her prayer the doxology at the end of the Eucharistic prayer: "Through him, with him, in him, in the unity of the Holy Spirit, all glory and honor is yours, almighty Father, forever and ever." Her work and her relationships with those who work with her are all caught up into her worship of God through Christ.

### THE TRANSCENDENT

While in our own times there is a great need to express our faith in an incarnational way, we also yearn to be in touch with the transcendent in worship. In the marketplace, work means achieving short-term goals, accomplishing projects within tight schedules and under pressure to perform. Liturgy puts our daily life struggles into a larger perspective. We see the "big picture," stretching from creation to the parousia. As an advertising executive told me, "The liturgy puts me in touch with tradition; I am given a sense of continuity with something and Someone beyond my narrow life and my immediate goals. I am refreshed, renewed, and above all refocused by the liturgy." Another executive said that he experienced this sense of tradition and continuity in his home parish where he had lived for twenty-five years and where the liturgy was celebrated with a certain dignity and grace. He contrasted it with a Newman Center where he occasionally worships. There he found that the liturgy was more like theater, a one-time media event, interesting and perhaps challenging, but not providing him with the sense of rootedness, mystery, and transcendence which he sought.

### THE COMMUNITY

The experience of the community at worship counters the pervasive individualism we experience in business. We cannot worship alone. Liturgy happens when a group of people gathers—old and young, black, yellow, white, brown, rich and poor, gay and straight, healthy and handicapped—to accomplish the work of the people of God. In song and prayer, in movement and ministry, we experience and act out our union with God and with each other. Having celebrated and acknowledged our human dignity and our solidarity within an inclusive worship community, we are

**Maria Leonard**

empowered to go out to live and work side by side with those who are different from ourselves.

The many people who use their talents and gifts in ministry for the common good are models for us in business. I am reminded especially of Ray who used his special training and skills as an actor to empower lectors to proclaim the Word. In business, professionals become mentors to younger workers, often sharing the wealth of their contacts and experience to help others.

Today, there is a great deal of discussion in management circles about the difference between managers and leaders. A whole body of literature is developing on the characteristics of the business person as leader. Leaders are described as charismatic persons who empower their colleagues, encouraging participation and delegating responsibility and decision-making to the lowest possible level. Such is the leadership required to implement the "new American experiment" proposed by the bishops in the Economics Pastoral. The experiment is to be a partnership for the public good, a partnership involving all levels of the economy, all actors and all peoples, even to the international level. The experiment is based on a spirit of cooperation derived from the solidarity and human dignity of all. This solidarity and its concomitant cooperative behavior flies in the face of the rugged individualism in our society and in our capitalistic way of life. Within the liturgy, the ministries of so many people model a different kind of relationship.

These examples illustrate the good things that happen when liturgy is celebrated well. Unfortunately, liturgy can also reinforce negative affections and attitudes.

ON THE MINUS SIDE

Several months ago, a first Mass was celebrated with twenty-five concelebrants. Some people dubbed the Mass a "coronation." There was no regard for a prior community decision against concelebrations for any occasion. Wouldn't a more humble beginning of ministry be appropriate, particularly as a minister of the Christ who was born in a stable and began his ministry with his baptism among sinners? Coincidentally, on the same day, Cardinal Bernardin celebrated Mass for the National Consultation of the Laity. In the assembly were hundreds of laity from throughout the United States, plus a bishop, some monsignors, and a sprinkling of priests, including the pastor of the church. The cardinal presided and led the assembly in worship, unassisted by concelebrants. In so doing, he clearly illustrated the role and function of the presider and the assembly and made visible the priesthood of the ordained and the priesthood of the laity. Which celebration supported the equal dignity of all people? Which celebration reflected elitism and modeled itself after the power states of executives in companies?

We must listen to what people say about their experience in liturgy, what the rites mean to them, how they are moved—if they are moved. With the best of intentions we may create attitudes and foster behavior diametrically opposed to those we intend, opposed to those of Christ. The liturgy has the power to shape us and our attitudes into the image of the risen Lord.

III. PRACTICAL MEANS FOR CONNECTING FAITH AND WORK
What can we do outside the liturgy to support people in the workplace? We can begin by reflecting as a group upon the relationship between faith and work. Any adult-education programming in parishes should include workshops or presentations on the vocation of the laity. The recent Synod on the Laity presented an ideal teaching moment and free publicity. Although the Synod focused more on internal Church issues rather than on the Church in the world, there was discussion in the Catholic press about both the internal and external mission of Catholics, as well as debate about where to place the emphasis.

The Economics Pastoral should be integrated into existing programs, activities, and institutions. The pastoral is not another program, but a vision and a way of living the economic dimension of our Christian life in the United States. Its principles should be incorporated into the Rite of Christian Initiation for Adults and confirmation classes, into high school religion programs, and in peace-and-justice committee work. Parish staffs, parish councils, and similar parish organizations should study the pastoral and reflect on ways to model its principles, especially those of human dignity, collaboration, equality, and preferential option for the poor. The United States Catholic Conference and diocesan peace-and-justice offices offer films, programs, and other resource materials to assist in implementing and teaching the principles of the pastoral. Call to Action in Chicago has developed a dramatic

**Maria Leonard**

and musical interpretation of the pastoral titled "Between the Times." Liturgy Training Publications has a fine booklet with selected quotations from both the Peace and the Economic Pastorals for each Sunday of the year. The booklet is designed to help teachers, homilists, and parish staffs. The carefully chosen texts may be used in homilies, as catalysts for preparing the general intercessions, as bulletin items, or as discussion points for catechetical sessions or religious-education programs.

A number of centers for business ethics have formed throughout the country. Some of these centers would be willing to present courses or provide lecturers. Many parishes support these ecumenical centers, and parishioners become involved in their programs and conferences.

In this age of peer counseling and support groups, probably the ideal way of making the connection between faith and work is within small groups of business people who meet for discussion and prayer. Groups are often headed by lay persons who set their own agenda.

Three years ago I began a group called "Christians in the Workplace" at St. Clement's parish. Initially, the group identified issues which they wanted to discuss. We also reflected on the Sunday readings, and I discussed the encyclical. The goal was to create a supportive environment in which those who work could reflect on the meaning of their work in the light of Scripture and Church teaching. The group also wanted ideas from each other on how to respond to criticism of the Church, how to solve difficult ethical or moral situations in business, and how to balance the demands of a career and personal life. Other topics included success, the meaning of power, and how to deal with put-downs on the job. We explored dilemmas such as how to influence and communicate equitable layoffs and terminations; how to respond to unethical requests from a supervisor; and to what extent one can discuss "God" in the workplace.

In the group, I found a hunger for an understanding of vocation and a search for meaning. When we talked of baptism and our union with Christ, our role as co-creators and co-redeemers, people responded with enthusiasm. One woman said, "Now I understand why you are so excited about the new baptismal font for the Church. I'm beginning to see what baptism means." Another woman who is a nurse said she saw her work in a totally new

**Work Week and Marketplace**

light. This surprised me because I was accustomed to think that most nurses looked upon their profession as a vocation.

Groups such as this one at my parish have sprung up in many places. Some have been started in companies, with employees meeting before work or at lunchtime. Some are for men or women only. Some are breakfast meetings in restaurants. Others have been formed for a variety of professional or occupational groups. Whether they begin with experience and move to interpret that experience in the light of theology, whether they are Bible study groups, or whether they have more open agendas, their underlying purpose is to help lay people find meaning in life, especially in work, and to be a support to one another. A lecture series called the First Friday Club of Chicago presents speakers of interest to business persons. In the first year, an average of two hundred people attended each luncheon held in a downtown hotel.

We are fortunate in Chicago to have a core of people who have made the role of the laity in the world the focal point of their mission in 1977, forty-seven people met at the University of Notre Dame and signed a Declaration of Christian Concern in which they argued that the role of the Christian in the world was being overlooked and devalued in Church circles. The National Center for the Laity was an outgrowth of that meeting. Last fall, the Center sponsored a national consultation to discuss the task of integrating faith with secular life in America. This spring, they sponsored a retreat, again for the laity, examining how and where one encounters Christ outside of the liturgy. The Center publishes an excellent newsletter, *Initiatives*. It includes information about programs and developments which support the Christian vocation in the world. Bill Droel, editor, along with Greg Pierce, staff member, also write a syndicated column, "Faith and Work," appearing in papers throughout the United States.

Most of these support groups have either been initiated by the laity or have involved the laity in formation and design. We Christians are, after all, a community of equal disciples; we are all learners on a journey. In addition, clergy and religious need to make an effort to understand the dynamics of the business world. That was the recommendation of the CEO who said he had only heard one sermon in his life on business.

Up to now, we have discussed programs and other experiences

**Maria Leonard**

168

which are essentially of an educational or deductive nature. We can also help people make the connection between faith and work through prayer. Common prayer may take the form of shared reflection on the Scriptures, evening or morning prayer with shared homily, or days or evenings of recollection. The focus of this prayer should be one's life, perhaps starting with one's own experiences of God's presence—moments of revelation or enlightenment—or the examination and interpretation of one's life in the light of faith. Personal prayer and reflection should also be taught and fostered. I often wonder how the ordinary Christian prays. What is the type of prayer which would help active Christians deepen their faith and discipleship? One man meditates on the daily Scripture readings. Another woman says morning and evening prayer from the Breviary. Many attend daily Mass. Another says the morning offering. Are there ways in which we can help people learn to pray? Do we need to develop a special type of prayer, different from the traditional monastic models?

CONCLUSION

Together we have walked down several paths trying to complete the circle of worship and life. We began with my novice friend telling me that my work was as important as my prayer. We then looked deep into the waters where we are all reborn and came away with a view of Christian vocation which is essentially our work. We examined how the liturgy shapes our attitudes and affections which in turn influence our behavior in the workplace. I outlined some practical, educational models for developing connections between faith and work. And finally, I have suggested that we need to learn to pray.

I believe that persons deeply involved in parish liturgy make their best contributions to the laity by preparing good liturgy and homilies which relate to the day-to-day life of the local community. In our liturgies and homilies, we need to help people come to an awareness of the unity between their daily lives and their vocation as Christians, twenty-four hours a day. We also need to find ways to explore the riches and implications of our baptism and try to bring together interested and knowledgeable men and women for discussion and prayer about the meaning of their work. We need to discover with them what their lives are about and what their needs are and then support them as they develop

**Work Week and Marketplace**

programs or processes to respond to those needs. This may seem like new mission territory, and for most of us, it is. We must think of ourselves as Francis Xaviers on their way to India, only India for us today is Wall Street or LaSalle Street or Main Street, U.S.A.

Maria Leonard

170